The Rape of Clarissa

For
Alan Ward

τὸν κρατοῦντα μαλθακῶς
θεὸς πρόσωθεν εὐμενῶς προσδέρκεται.

The Rape of Clarissa

Writing, Sexuality and Class Struggle in Samuel Richardson

TERRY EAGLETON

University of Minnesota Press · Minneapolis

Published by the University of Minnesota Press,
2037 University Avenue Southeast, Minneapolis MN 55414
Printed in Great Britain

ISBN 0-8166-1204-8
0-8166-1209-9 (pbk)

The University of Minnesota is an equal-opportunity
educator and employer.

Contents

Preface

The German critic Walter Benjamin dismissed the view that all literary works were equally 'readable' at all times. For Benjamin, a work may fall into obscurity for centuries, only to be suddenly reactivated as the history to which it belongs flashes into freshly relevant relationship to our own epoch. The task of criticism, as Benjamin saw it, was to 'blast open the continuum of history', forging conjunctures between our own moment and a redeemed bit of the past, imbuing works with retroactive significance so that in them we may better read the signs of our own times.[1]

The wager of this book is that it is just possible that we may now once again be able to read Samuel Richardson. This was not on the whole possible for the nineteenth century, for which Coleridge's damning judgement was largely decisive: 'His mind is so very vile a mind, so oozy, so hypocritical, praise-mad, canting, envious, concupiscent.'[2] It would seem an unenviable task to try and redeem *that*. Yet Coleridge's remark was made in the context of admiration; and there are those who have claimed *Clarissa* as the greatest English novel. Though I suppose one should be sceptical of such transcendental judgements, it may still

1 See my *Walter Benjamin, or Towards a Revolutionary Criticism* (London, 1981), especially part 2, 3.
2 *Anima Poetae* (London, 1895), p. 166.

be the case that *Clarissa* can now become a great novel for us. If this happens, it will be because certain new ways of reading developed in our own time, closely related to the nature of our own history and to the political interests of a Richardson, have made his texts available in a new way.

There are three such methods of reading conjointly used in this book. The first arises from the various post-structuralist theories of textuality, of vital relevance to an author as obsessed as Richardson was by the act of writing. The second is a feminist and psychoanalytical perspective: if Richardson may once again become readable, it will be in large measure because of the women's movement. Two facts in particular seem to have denied *Clarissa* recognition as arguably the major feminist text of the language. The first is that, greatest English novel or not, it is certainly the longest, and so has been little read; the second is that its author was male. Whether my account of the novel can outweigh these embarrassments is for the reader to decide; I would be glad enough if the book simply served to make people want to read Richardson and argue with my case. As for psychoanalysis, I suppose I must apologize for entering upon this terrain, which the English have always found a little unnerving. It is customary for Richardson critics to tip their hats gravely in the direction of the un-conscious; it is simply any systematic spelling out of the matter that they seem to find a little indecent.

The book's third method is that of historical material-ism. The contemporary resurgence of Marxist criticism, with its interest not only in class struggle but in literary modes of production, is another factor which might allow us to read Richardson with new insight. The eighteenth century has long been the preserve of literary conservatism, rarely penetrated by Marxist criticism, and one purpose of my book is accordingly to appropriate a little of this patch. My second apology, then, is that I entirely lack what would appear to be one of the chief credentials for discussing the eighteenth century, namely a nostalgic urge to return to it. I am not out to suggest that Richardson was a radical even in his own society's terms, let alone in ours; much of his ideology strikes me as repellent and irredeemable. I am concerned rather with his position as intellectual and literary producer within an emergent class, and with what socialists — for whom that class is today the enemy — may learn from that location. But I am also concerned with what seem to me the genuinely subversive effects of *Clarissa*, which far exceed its author's intentions.

I am particularly grateful to Toril Moi, whose influence on this book is deep and pervasive.

T. E.

Introduction

Samuel Richardson was born, appropriately enough, in 1689, one year after the 'Glorious Revolution' that laid the foundations of bourgeois democracy in England, one year before the appearance of the great manifesto of that settlement, Locke's *Two Treatises of Government*, and exactly one century before the rather more turbulent establishment of such a state in revolutionary France. By the end of the seventeenth century, the English bourgeoisie, in alliance with the more 'progressive' landed gentry, had dismantled the absolutist state of the Stuarts and fashioned a political framework for the intensive accumulation of capital. The sway of feudalist aristocracy in England had been decisively overthrown: although the aristocracy retained social and political dominance, with many of its familiar institutions surviving intact, the economic directions of the society had been irreversibly altered.

Writing of a later stage of class struggle, the Italian Marxist Antonio Gramsci argued that any revolutionary class, in addition to seizing political power, must secure *cultural* hegemony over its opponents. To seal its victory, such a class must do more than break the political, military and juridical strength of its oppressors, crushing their armies and transforming their state; it must also challenge and oust them in the realms of religion, philosophy, art, morality, language and manners. Its conquests must stretch beyond the visible areas of parliaments, law courts and industrial production to the more elusive textures of human subjectivity: everyday habits and values, assumptions and affections, practices and perceptions. Only in this way would a revolution produce not just a new society, but a new human subject equipped to inhabit it. A revolution which can transform modes of production but not types of speech, social relations but not styles of architecture, remains radically incomplete. The process of political change, then, must be coupled with a practice of 'cultural revolution' — a fierce conflict over signs and meanings, as the newly emergent class strives to wrest the most cherished symbols from the grip of its rivals and redefine them in its own image.

At the forefront of such cultural revolution stand those whom Gramsci terms the 'organic' intellectuals: those writers, political leaders and theoreticians who are themselves products of the rising social class rather than remnants of the old.[1] Brought to unwonted prominence by the upheavals of history, tied to the progressive class by personal as well as ideological bonds, this 'organic' intelligentsia will do more than reflect the interests of those for whom it speaks: it will prove an active force in the very framing of such interests, shaping them into a 'world view' rich and coherent enough to challenge the dominant ideology. Marked out from the 'traditional' intelligentsia by deep differences of style, origin and status, the organic intellectuals become a focus in which the new class may find its fragmentary impulses united, a medium in which it achieves self-consciousness.

Samuel Richardson, who believed that tradesmen 'are infinitely of more consequence, and deserve more to be

---

1 *Selections from the Prison Notebooks*, ed. Q. Hoare and G. Nowell-Smith (London, 1971), pp. 452–3.

incourag'd, than any other degree or rank of people',[2] was not only one such organic intellectual of the English bourgeoisie; he was among the most vitally significant of all. The son of a Derbyshire joiner, with perhaps only a year or so of secondary education, almost no classical learning and a relatively narrow acquaintance with the literature of his own society, Richardson passed his placidly uneventful life largely outside the circles of metropolitan literary culture, as a gauche self-made businessman dogged by feelings of social inferiority.[3] He rose from printer's apprentice to become one of London's leading printers, employing by his own account thirty to forty men, and widely respected throughout his profession; yet though his novels were to become a byword from Napoleon to Pushkin, Rousseau to de Sade, Goethe to Blake, he remained more concerned with disciplining his apprentices than discussing fine art. Untravelled and inarticulate, utterly commonplace in his middle-class puritan opinions, Richardson not only dramatically transformed the course of English fiction and left an indelible impress on world literature; in doing so, he played a key role in the English class struggle.

Gramsci's model must, of course, be modified for English history, where we do things rather differently. In eighteenth-century England, no mortal combat took place between nobility and bourgeoisie; in the wake of

2 Quoted by T. C. Duncan Eaves and Ben K. Kimpel, *Samuel Richardson: A Biography* (Oxford, 1971), p. 542. Throughout this book I have modernized the eighteenth-century use of the capital letter.

3 Richardson was by no means entirely without friends in high cultural places. Visiting him one day, Hogarth came across a man convulsively shaking his head and rolling about, who must be, he decided, 'an ideot, whom his relations had put under the care of Mr Richardson, as a very good man' (quoted by Eaves and Kimpel, *Samuel Richardson*, p. 336). The man was in fact Samuel Johnson.

seventeenth-century revolution, the middle class was content to shelter peacefully behind the insignia of traditional society, negotiating an ideological alliance with its social superiors. Richardson's fiction stands at the centre of this new discursive formation: it enacts what Brian W. Downs has called 'Steele's dual programme, the Christianizing of the wits and the polishing of the puritans'.[4] But that alliance could not be forged without virulent aggression. If the bourgeoisie was happy to preserve or tactfully modify certain aristocratic values, it was equally intent on curbing or uprooting certain others, resolved to saturate the whole ruling ideology with its own influence. Its relation to the aristocracy, like Richardson's own curious psychological blend of mildness and militancy, was sado-masochistic: humbly submissive to gentility, it savaged luxury and licentiousness; bowed to the sacredness of social hierarchy, it vigorously affirmed its individualism.

It would be easy, and relatively unoriginal, to show how Richardson's novels are among other things great allegories of class warfare, narratives of alliance and antagonism between a predatory nobility and a pious bourgeoisie. For the moment, however, I am interested less in what that fiction 'mirrors' than in what it *does*. For Richardson's novels are not mere images of conflicts fought out on another terrain, representations of a history which happens elsewhere; they are themselves a material part of those struggles, pitched standards around which battle is joined, instruments which help to constitute social interests rather than lenses which reflect them. These novels are an agent, rather than mere account, of the English bourgeoisie's attempt to wrest a degree of ideological hegemony from the aristocracy in the decades which follow the political settlement of 1688. Pamela, Clarissa and Sir Charles Grandison are not only fictional characters: they are also

4   *Richardson* (London, 1928), p. 168.

public mythologies, coordinates of a mighty moral debate, symbolic spaces within which dialogues may be conducted, pacts concluded and ideological battle waged. *Pamela*, one of the century's best sellers, was less a 'novel' than a pass-word or badge of allegiance, code for what became in effect a whole cultural event: 'Fashionable ladies displayed copies in public places, and held fans painted with pictures of its best-loved scenes. *Pamela* became a play, an opera, even a waxwork; and in a society suspicious of fiction had the distinction of a recommendation from a London pulpit.'[5] The modern equivalent of *Pamela* would not be *Mrs Dalloway* but a phenomenon like Superman.[6] The literary text — *Superman* comic itself — is merely the occasion or organizing principle of a multimedia affair, stretching all the way from domestic commodities to public spectacles, instantly recodable from one cultural mode to the next. Like Superman, *Pamela* is the name for a diverse set of social practices, an emblem encountered at every turn, a domestic talking-point and public declaration of faith. The literary text is not merely to be read: it is to be dramatized, displayed, wielded as cultural totem, ransacked for moral propaganda or swooned over as love story, preached from the pulpit and quoted in the salons. Pamela, Clarissa and Grandison are public property subject to strategic uses, lynchpins of an entire ideological formation. Around the fictions they inhabit, an enormous body of writing begins to proliferate: letters to and from the author, savage spoofs and denunciatory pamphlets, bawdy rhymes and poetic encomiums, imitations and translations. *Pamela* is pirated, put into heroic couplets, adapted for the

5 Mark Kinkead-Weekes, Introduction to the Everyman edition of *Pamela* (London, 1966), p. v.

6 The more obviously appropriate analogy — Superwoman — misses the pervasiveness of *Pamela*'s effects, perfunctory appendage as she is to her male precursor.

stage by Voltaire and Goldoni, inscribed in its French edition on the Roman Catholic Index. If Richardson's characters are no more confined to their official texts than Superman, they also transcend purely textual status in a way more akin to the protagonists of such modern sagas as *The Archers* or *Coronation Street*. An English village is reported to have rung its church bells on learning that Pamela was married; a devotee of *Clarissa*, who pronounced the novel the best tragedy since Adam, was helped to die peacefully by the heroine's example. Suspended between fact and fiction, Richardson's characters come to assume the ambiguous aura of myth, that symbolic realm so utterly paradigmatic that we can never quite decide whether it is more or less 'real' than the empirical world.

Richardson's novels, then, are not only or even primarily literary texts: they entwine with commerce, religion, theatre, ethical debate, the visual arts, public entertainment. They are both cogs in a culture industry and sacred scripture to be reverently conned. In short, they are organizing forces of what, after German political theory, we may term the bourgeois 'public sphere'.[7] The eighteenth-century middle class must do more than amass capital or trade in titles: its moral power must permeate the textures of civil society, pitting the values of thrift, peace and chastity against a violent and profligate nobility. Emboldened by its political and economic advances, it is now emerging from the privacy of business and bedroom to impress its ideology on society as a whole. It must carve out a space for itself in the domain of public discourse, furnished with its own distinctive style and rhetoric, equipped with its own journals, presses, manners, meeting places, techniques of cultural production. In one sense,

7 See Jürgen Habermas, *Strukturwandel der Öffentlichkeit* (Neuwied, 1962).

such an emergent culture may be said to form a 'counter-public sphere' to aristocratic power, equivalent to what we might imagine possible for the progressive social class of our own time. To oppose and undermine bourgeois culture, the contemporary working-class movement would equally require its own presses and journals, theatres and television stations, festivals and assembly halls. But if this culture were to form more than a defensive enclave within capitalism, it would also need to make constant aggressive inroads into the bourgeois public sphere, confronting the contemporary ruling class on its own terrain.

Richardson did not only share in the bourgeois public sphere of eighteenth-century England; he helped to construct it. He did so not only by his writing, but by fashioning a whole social apparatus. What would be the ideal location for an organic intellectual of his kind? He would need to live in close touch with the flourishing economic life of the class he represented. He would seek to share in the framing of its political interests. He would strive to intervene constantly in the everyday culture of his class, forming taste, charting trends and disseminating doctrine. He would require access to its major ideological channels, placing himself at the heart of ethical controversies, educational projects, religious and aesthetic contentions. As master printer, Richardson achieved all of these goals at a stroke. His printing firm was of course a thriving capitalist enterprise, locked into the economic infrastructure of bourgeois England. But it was also the centre of a vast ideological network, the nub of a whole discursive formation. This single print works off Fleet Street, set in an undistinguished precinct of petty-bourgeois tradespeople (victuallers, tallow chandlers, periwig-makers and the like), interlocked with every major ideological apparatus of English society. From it, Richardson produced a series of journals, among them the main political organ of the Walpole government, which ranged in content from 'theoretical ideology' to problems of popular culture. Defences of Walpole and polemics against slavery were juxtaposed with remedies for haemorrhoids and halitosis,[8] literary reviews and critiques of deism set beside commentaries on bankruptcy law and public house licensing. For the emergent English bourgeoisie, as for the socialist movement of our own epoch, the frontier between 'political' and 'cultural' discourse was constantly transgressed. If Richardson's print works sank its roots into the most inconspicuous crevices of middle-class culture, it also extended its feelers into the most august of state ideological apparatuses. Richardson was printer to the House of Commons, and later in life statute and law printer to the king, with a half-share of an exclusive right to print all books dealing with common law. Nor were the academic institutions omitted: Richardson was one of three printers employed by the Society for the Encouragement of Learning, and was later to become printer to the Royal Society. The relation between his business and that other dominant ideological form — religion — is, of course, self-evident: though he was by no means averse to a sound profit, that motive took second place to the nurturing of Christian virtue through print.

Political, pedagogic, religious, cultural and juridical: Richardson's firm moved at the intersection of these

8 Richardson had a reason to interest himself in patent medicines, being for most of his life in fairly bad health. The favoured remedy of his physician, George Cheyne, was a good vomit. 'Your short neck is rather an argumt. for a vomit now and then than against it for no long necked animal can vomit, and vomits are the best preservative from apoplexies after little phlebotomies' (quoted by Eaves and Kimpel, *Samuel Richardson*, p. 63). Cheyne also recommended Richardson to drink a tincture of soot in peppermint water in order to make him 'break wind plentifully', and persuaded him to work strapped in a sort of rocking chair, so that he could have a good bounce while reading or dictating. Cheyne died sixteen months after recommending this health cure.

mighty ideological apparatuses. Yet if it was in this sense a switchboard of some great impersonal system of significations, it was modelled, paradoxically, on that most interpersonal of all ideological institutions, the family. For most of his working life, Richardson more or less literally lived above the shop; part of his business was actually installed in his private dwelling. His firm never grew large enough to outstrip his personal supervision, and the traditional quasi-paternal relationship between master printer and apprentices blurred any hard distinction between the domestic and the industrial. The effect of this situation is curious. 'Samuel Richardson' denotes a powerhouse of vital ideological interests, a discursive formation which enmeshes English society, connects with its power structures and spreads to catch the sensibility of Europe in its sway. Yet the man Samuel Richardson remains shadowily inaccessible, a self-effacing entrepreneur in some ways more akin to the periwig-makers of his precinct than to the mighty whom his fictions enthralled. This paradox is rooted in the nature of the printing industry: in the discrepancy between its artisanal techniques of production and its ramifying ideological effects. The book devotedly produced by a few skilled workers becomes an anonymous commodity with unfathomable consequences. But it is also an incongruity which we shall find echoed in Richardson's novels. What threatens to proliferate beyond personal control in his writing is nothing less than *writing itself*. It is writing — that sprawling mesh of dangerously open-ended signs — which Richardson and his characters strive to leash to a personal intention. The patriarch of his print works, Richardson is also sole progenitor of his texts; it is not fortuitous that the terms in which he discusses his relationship to his own writing are at times those of dominance and aggression. Yet texts, like apprentices, may be wayward and insubordinate, subject to piracy and rape;[9] the phrase *master printer* has an oxymoronic ring to it, suggesting authority over the perpetually insubordinate, proprietorship of that which is nobody's property. There is a tension in Richardson's very place within material production, between local artisan and international ideologue, which becomes figured in the form of his work.

The most interesting meaning of *family* in Richardson, however, stretches beyond his wife, children and workers. When Lady Davers writes to Pamela that 'you have made us a family of readers and writers',[10] the same could be affirmed of Richardson by his audience. Richardson's true family, it might be claimed, is his social class — more particularly, those of its representatives who collaborated in the production of his fictions. He never, to be sure, took much of the literary advice he so doggedly sought, remaining master printer in this sense too; but his writing nevertheless springs from a mode of cultural production more akin to the collective, open-ended, revisionary strategies of modern 'epic' theatre than it is to the modern novel. He sent the manuscript of *Clarissa* in frequent lengthy instalments to his friend Aaron Hill for editing, and circulated it constantly among friends during its three or so years' gestation; as the volumes appeared, critical correspondence about the novel's progress and desirable outcome rapidly mounted, and a postscript to the final volume addresses itself directly to readers' responses. Richardson wrote comments on Lady Bradshaigh's comments on *Pamela* and *Clarissa*, and solicited a preface from William Warburton (whom he had invited to correct *Pamela*) to some volumes of the first edition of *Clarissa*. He incorporated into the third and fourth editions of *Clarissa* an anonymously donated collection of its moral

9 See Eaves and Kimpel, *Samuel Richardson*, pp. 377–83, for an account of an Irish pirating of *Sir Charles Grandison*.
10 *Pamela* (London, 1966), vol. 2, p. 34.

sentiments, duly revised and enlarged by himself. Collaboration around *Sir Charles Grandison* was even more
intensive: Richardson invited his women friends to contri-
bute scenes and prefaces, occasionally showed them each
other's critical comments, and entrusted overall criticism
and correction of the manuscript to the religious author
Catherine Talbot. Pressed to produce a sequel to the novel,
he toyed with the notion of assembling a fully collective
text: his critical correspondents were to assume the roles
of the various characters left surviving from *Grandison*,
sending him material which he would edit into a complete
work.[11]

The collaborative nature of Richardson's writing may,
of course, be dismissed as personal quirk (some authors
habitually seek advice, others do not), or as vanity: he
enjoyed soliciting the views of the famous female coterie
to whom he read his works aloud, in a kind of teasing
erotic play. But the famous female coterie, for long the
malicious sport of the male critics, was for the most part
a group of perceptive, well-educated, critically astute
women; and Richardson's compact with them is best seen
as a crucial act of solidarity. It was no mere avuncular
masochist who sent copies of *Pamela* to Aaron Hill's
daughters with interleaved pages for their corrections.
Richardson is concerned no more than Bertolt Brecht
with the sleek literary product alone; like Brecht, he is
preoccupied with the material *practice* of writing, the
potentially endless process of wrangles and revisions, the
complex business of circulating drafts, conflating criticisms

11 Richardson was not above a little bribery in this respect: he
asked his friend Hester Mulso to produce a letter from Clementina to
Harriet, and as a *quid pro quo* generously offered to let her marry
Clementina to the Count. On receiving letters from two young
women about Clarissa, one accusing her of prudery and the other
of coquettishness, he sent each woman's letter to the other.

of criticisms, initiating dialogues and establishing friendships. Richardson's life is his literary work, not his literary works. In creating this partially collective mode of literary production, he turns his texts into pretexts — into occasions for sharply nuanced debate, forums for continuous mutual education, media for social rituals and relations. He produced, not simply a set of novels, but a whole society in miniature; by sustaining a constant circulation of discourse, a potentially infinite generation of texts about texts, he converted the process of his art into an act of ideological solidarity. It was not, however, mindless consensus: fervent discussions around the gradually evolving Clarissa or Grandison, anguished contentions over their desirable destinies, became modes of ever finer ideological formulation, scrupulous probings of precise meanings. Transforming the production as well as consumption of his works into a social practice, Richardson half-converts himself from 'author' to the focal point of his readers' own writings. Yet text and pretext are not easily separable. The literary reception of his novels, as manuscripts pass from hand to hand and the flurry of letters increases, becomes an integral moment of their production, a constitutive force rather than retrospective response. The Richardsonian text, like the Brechtian theatre script, can never be definitive: it lives only as a function of audience feedback or authorial second thoughts, fruits of a wider social discourse from which it is inseparable. It is in this sense, as well as in the technical meaning he himself intended, that Richardson's writing is 'to the moment'.

Within his novels, to be sure, *family* has its usual designation, as the central apparatus of patriarchal society.[12] But the sense of *family* which produces those fictions

---

12 I use the term 'patriarchy' throughout this book in a broad sense, to mean male-dominated society, rather than in a more technical, and perhaps more proper, sense.

undermines, in however modest and implicit a form, that privileged meaning. For Richardson, ideology is thicker than blood: his 'family' is one constructed by literary practice, not genetically given. Stretching from his few intimate fellow writers and circle of women friends to his numerous correspondents, it widens to become effectively coextensive with the 'public sphere' of which he is spokesman. Within the extended family of his female coterie, Richardson certainly remains the smugly ensconced patriarch, trading a mildly eroticized banter for an agreeable flattery; there is little doubt that, wittingly or not, he exploits his literary powers to tighten his hold over women. Yet what he thereby fashions as a social form is also a kind of alternative to the patriarchal family, in which what counts is neither 'blood' nor sexual property but acumen and sensibility. His securely sublimated relationship with his women friends reproduces a father–daughter relationship at the same time as it challenges sexual power relations in the name of a certain comradeship. It is true that the coterie served to canonize women in their role as specialists in sentiment; but it is also true that such sentiment, with what may be called the bourgeois 'feminization of discourse', was now playing a more vitally constitutive part in the male public sphere. In a contradictory movement, 'feminine' values relegated by the sexual division of labour to the private realm are now returning to transvaluate the ruling ideologies themselves. The feminization of discourse prolongs the fetishizing of women at the same time as it lends them a more authoritative voice. If Richardson's coterie travesties women as technicians of the heart, it is also a mechanism which partly readmits them to the public sphere.

'You must see,' Richardson wrote to Lady Bradshaigh, 'that the tendency of all I have written is to exalt the sex.'[13]

---

13 *Selected Letters of Samuel Richardson*, ed. with an Introduction by John Carroll (Oxford, 1964), p. 112.

He is not, as we shall see, quite the ardent feminist this makes him sound; but his writing is nevertheless part of a deep-seated 'feminization' of values throughout the eighteenth century which is closely allied with the emergence of the bourgeoisie. The decline of the relatively open, impersonal system of traditional kinship, with its primarily economic and genealogical rather than affective bonds, has produced by Richardson's era a considerably more closed, 'nuclear' family, whose patriarchal structure reinforces an authoritarian state and fulfils some of the religious functions traditionally performed by the church.[14] The other face of this despotic patriarchy is a deepening of emotional ties between men and women, the emergence of new forms of subjectivity of which the birth of 'childhood',[15] the hymning of spiritual companionship within marriage and the proliferating cults of 'sentiment' and 'sensibility' are major signs. Jean H. Hagstrum has tracked this veritable paradigm shift in the ideology of gender from its radical puritan source in the works of John Milton.[16] A doughty defender of patriarchy, Milton nonetheless threatens that ideology with his subversive plea for rational friendship and mutual love in marriage; and the stage is then set for John Dryden, who 'created within a belligerent heroic world characters moved by delicate love, tender pity, and soft compassion'.[17] Addison, Steele and Defoe are eighteenth-century inheritors of this elevation of the 'feminine', and Samuel Richardson its most gifted and popular ideologue. By the time of Sir Charles

14 See Lawrence Stone, *The Family, Sex and Marriage in England 1500–1800* (Harmondsworth, 1979), chapter 5.
15 See Philippe Ariès, *Centuries of Childhood* (London, 1962), especially part 3.
16 See his *Sex and Sensibility: Ideal and Erotic Love from Milton to Mozart* (Chicago and London, 1980).
17 ibid., p. 50.

Grandison, a wholesale 'domestication of heroism'[18] has been effected: the barbarous values of militarism, naked dominance and male *hauteur*, badges of a predatory public aristocracy, have been mollified by the fashionable virtues of uxoriousness, sensibility, civility and *tendresse*.[19] Pity, pathos and the pacific, 'womanly' qualities suppressed by a warring nobility, become the hallmarks of a bourgeoisie whose economic goals seem best guaranteed by political tranquillity. Possessive individualism and Protestant ideology entail a new 'turn to the subject', inseparable from the 'nuclear' reorganizing of the family. In bourgeois philosophy, a militant empiricism discredits the coldly rational and embraces the raw stuff of subjective sensation. Post-Lockeian political theory, distressed by the sectarianism of civil war, espouses a 'moderation' more traditionally associated with the mildness of women than with the aggression of men. Appalled by upper-class brutality, a socially reformist bourgeoisie unfurls the banner of humanitarian benevolence, spurred by its historical triumphs to a sanguine trust in human goodness.

Having artificially constructed a powerless, ghettoized 'feminine' culture, then, English class society in the eighteenth century begins to reintegrate such values, exploiting them to fashion a new ideological formation. The 'exaltation' of women, while undoubtedly a partial advance in itself, also serves to shore up the very system which oppresses them. For the eighteenth-century woman, as indeed for women of any epoch, the pedestal is never very far from the pit. It is arguable that the material conditions of middle- and upper-class women improved in some ways over the century: the property rights of wives were more protected, and women were generally expected

18 ibid., p. 214.
19 See R. F. Brissenden, *Virtue in Distress: Studies in the Novel of Sentiment from Richardson to Sade* (London, 1974).

to be better educated.[20] But the nuclear family which lent them greater affective status also brutally isolated them from the protection of an extended kinship, cloistered them from the public sphere and reduced them to delicate drones. If the burgeoning ideology of romantic love loosened the constraints of patriarchy, with its respect for the child's individual choice of a marriage partner, it also emotionally blackmailed the woman into even deeper bondage to her husband. 'The pretence of affection,' complains Defoe's Roxana, 'takes from a woman everything that can be called herself: She is to have no interest, no aim, no view, but all is the interest, aim and view of the husband. She is to be the passive creature.'[21] Richardson writes at a transitional point in this history, where a growing regard for the free affections of the subject deadlocks with a still vigorous patriarchal tyranny. If the general eighteenth-century trend was towards the rights of women in choosing their husbands, *Clarissa* would suggest that older patriarchal attitudes were still lethally active. It is because that novel is produced at a transitional point that it can dramatize the contradictions of ruling-class patriarchy as vividly as it does. Though the source of the 'novel of sentiment', *Clarissa* is not exactly one itself: the term *sentiments* to Richardson would have meant something like 'moral views' rather than 'tender feelings'.[22] *Clarissa*, in other words, predates the triumph of the affective, subjectivist sense of *sentiment*; individual sensibility has not yet carried all before it, but is tragically at odds with a grimly impersonal power structure. Indeed R. F. Brissenden reads Lovelace, and the whole novel, as a drastic demystification of sentimentalist ideology,[23] a

20 See Stone, *The Family, Sex and Marriage in England,* pp. 167 and 232.
21 Quoted ibid., p. 249.
22 See Brissenden, *Virtue in Distress,* pp. 98f.
23 ibid., p. 35.

violent defacing of the myths of 'natural goodness' with which a benevolently weeping bourgeoisie concealed from itself its own exploitative practice.

Richardson's distinctive mode of literary production was only possible in a society without our own rigorous articulation of discourse into 'fictional' and 'non-fictional'. For though Pamela, Clarissa and Grandison never existed, nothing could be more insistently real than the ideological practices to which they give rise. The national crisis which Clarissa's death seems to have triggered is not to be ascribed to the heart-flutterings of gullible females; it is a measure of the material urgency of the themes which that death embodies. By turning his 'imaginative' products into real social processes, deploying fiction to organize new social relations, Richardson converted the still indeterminate status of the novel to effective ideological use. His calculated hesitancy between fact and fiction is more than a generic muddle; it belongs to a fruitful crisis in the whole problem of literary representation. The term *fiction*, let alone the contemptible *novel*, is ideologically impermissible − not because of some puritan neurosis about lying, but because it would seem merely to devalue the reality of the issues at stake. There is nothing 'novel' about *Clarissa*: this is no trashy escapism, no idle 'imaginative' creation, but the true history of women's oppression at the hands of eighteenth-century patriarchy. If it is 'imaginative', it is not particularly more so than Gibbon or Burke. It is true that Clarissa Harlowe never existed, but not important. As the fruit of certain dialogues and source of certain effects, Clarissa is, as it were, real enough to be going on with. It is because such characters are fictional that literary collaboration becomes possible: because their destinies are not carved in rock but open in principle to others' revisions, they evoke the real scriptive acts of Richardson's anxious friends. Since those friends do not 'believe' in Clarissa, they 'believe' in her all the more devoutly. Reading mimetic fiction is perhaps a paradigm case of the ambiguities of 'belief': Richardson himself speaks of 'that kind of historical faith, which fiction itself is generally read (with), even tho' we know it to be fiction'.[24] It certainly seems possible to believe and disbelieve something simultaneously, and an enquiry into the mechanisms of this might tell us more about the workings of ideologies. One reason why ideologies appear difficult to falsify is that they depend less on empirical than on 'exemplary' belief. A particular empirically falsifiable proposition is less an object of belief in itself than the occasion for a general 'set' towards the world; if it ceases to be empirically plausible, it may therefore be transformed into another proposition without damage to that general structure. At the same time, however, ideologies strive to hold us at the level of the local and immediate; by enthralling us to the particular, they seek to forestall the 'wrong' kind of generalization from it.

It would be possible to draw up an historical typology of fiction in the light of this model. At one end of the historical spectrum, myth and allegory would seem forms in which the empirical units are arbitrary and easily permutated, systems which allow for a degree of free play between general 'set' and specific elements. At the other end of the spectrum, modernist fiction exploits the arbitrariness of its particular units to unmask the brutal truth that they can be exemplary of whatever equally relative world view you care to conjure from them. Kafka is perhaps best read as recycling the former mode into the latter: the traditional world of allegory, in which each item seems free to combine with others to confirm a general vision, has become the modernist nightmare of Hegel's 'bad infinity', in which all the pieces are at once oppressively meaningful and sinisterly resistant to an 'exemplary' reading. What happens in between is realist fiction, caught in a cleft stick between its local persuasiveness and generalizing force. For if such fiction is to convince us of general truths, it must do so by the plausibility of its contingent details; yet the more it weaves these into a rich tapestry of 'lived experience', the more it endangers their exemplary status. It is a problem of which Samuel Richardson was perfectly aware. *Pamela* is passed off as a genuine collection of letters; that pretence is then dropped in *Clarissa*, but Richardson is still not announced as the author. Such ambiguity is tactically essential: Richardson writes to Warburton that he wants nothing in the preface which would *prove* the text to be fictional, but does not wish it to be *thought* genuine either, since this would weaken its exemplary force.[25] If *Clarissa* is taken as real it may be received as simply one more history, without representative value, and the whole ideological project would be accordingly scuppered. Yet if the reader is alerted in advance to its fictionality, the work will suffer in 'experiential' power. By the time of the preface to *Grandison*, Richardson is still officially pretending that his text is genuine but taking no pains to make the pretence plausible; he is, as it were, pretending to pretend. The hesitancy between history and fiction encodes the ideological dilemma of the realist novel: the paradox that its grounding in a supposed 'referent' is at once source and inhibition of its ideological efficacy. But this aporia can also be turned to duplicitous ends: by *suspending* his text between history and fable, Richardson seeks the best of all possible ideological worlds.

25 ibid.

The dense realism of *Pamela* and *Clarissa* is sustained by an allegorical structure, but the reader must not choose between them: without realism the allegory is empty, without allegory the realism is blind. Such texts demand a double reading, whereby psychological empathy coexists with 'exemplary' insight. It is not surprising that some modern critics of Richardson, nervous of the realist history, have sought to reduce his fiercely political fiction to the comfortingly recurrent 'archetypes' of myth.[26]

If Richardson's texts are not 'novels' in his own dismissive use of the term, neither are they novels in our own sense. A novel today is usually a finished, seamless product; Richardson's works, by contrast, are more usefully thought of as *kits*, great unwieldly containers crammed with spare parts and agreeable extras, for which the manufacturer never ceases to churn out new streamlined improvements, ingenious additions and revised instruction sheets. The second edition of *Pamela* comes complete with a table of contents intended to sharpen the moral, added footnotes, and some revised and appended passages. Later editions of *Clarissa* turn up furnished with supposedly 'restored' (in fact freshly written) material, and Richardson will later publish these passages as a separate volume. Clarissa's religious meditations, along with her author's commentary, are collected and printed for various friends; her most notable sentiments are likewise gathered in and printed, along with a brief index to them, at the end of the book.

26 William Hazlitt noted with characteristic acuteness that Richardson's novels 'have the romantic air of a pure fiction, with the literal minuteness of a common diary' ('Lectures on the Comic Writers', *The Complete Works of William Hazlitt*, ed. P. P. Howe (London and Toronto, 1931), vol. 6, pp. 117–18). For examples of the 'mythification' of Richardson, see Leslie Fiedler, *Love and Death in the American Novel* (New York, 1960; London, 1970), and Norman Rabkin, '*Clarissa:* A Study in the Nature of Convention', *English Literary History* 23, 1956.

One text ceaselessly spawns another, until the triumphant arrival of what one might have considered the key to all mythologies: the publication in 1755 of *A Collection of the Moral and Instructive Sentiments, Maxims, Cautions, and Reflexions, Contained in the Histories of Pamela, Clarissa, and Sir Charles Grandison.* Yet even this *summa* is no mere transcription of the original texts: passages are thoroughly rewritten and fresh sentiments added, a preface and appendix supplied, and the whole volume alphabetically arranged. Having completed this labour, Richardson turned in his latter years to arranging, censoring and indexing his voluminous correspondence for publication — that is to say, reworking texts written about his texts into a new text. He kept up a ceaseless revision of his works (radically so in the case of *Pamela*) until his death, at which point he abandoned writing altogether.

Prefaces, introductory letters, footnotes, appendices, indexes, postscripts, tables of contents: it would be tempting to see these as the 'outworks' of a Richardson novel, detachable from the entrenched fortress of the text itself. Yet the whole of the 'text itself' is also detachable, always capable of being worked loose from its original, which was probably no more than a revision of a revision in the first place. The whole of this dangerously labile writing is merely one enormous spare part, permanently capable of being recycled into something else. Constantly in motion 'in itself', Richardson's text is rocked into further instability by the 'supplementary' material added to ballast it. For that material is not, of course, '*hors texte*': in offering to 'explicate' Richardson's meaning, it finds itself sucked along by the whole turbulent textual process. 'Restorations' turn out to be addenda, 'addenda' attempt to plug textual gaps, textual gaps are created by 'restorations'. It is perhaps fortunate for Richardson that there was always death to part him from his pen.

Richardson's plural, diffuse kits of fiction belong with

his collaborative mode of literary production. This flexible, deconstructed apparatus can accommodate others' texts alongside his own, expand to encompass revisionary material, adapt to account for the latest critical feedback. The looseness of these fictions inscribes within them the mode of their making. In this sense their modern analogue would be less a novel than a newspaper — or, to revert to a previous parallel, the creaking machinery of 'epic' theatre, with its disarticulated structure and modifiable parts, its multiple, adaptive functions. If Richardson writes before fictional realism has been formalized, epic theatre happens when it has run its course. But there is a rather more obvious parallel between the two genres: both are un-ashamedly didactic. Richardson springs from an ascendant bourgeoisie; epic theatre is an art form of the militant working class. The most pressing problem for both forms can then be posed as follows: how is a structural openness, the essential medium of transformed relations between producers and audiences, to be reconciled with a necessary doctrinal closure?

Such closure is surely for us the unacceptable face of Samuel Richardson. It is the oozy canting prig who has been remembered, the high-minded hypocrite and prurient pedlar of pieties.[27] The Richardson who disseminates his writing to the winds, the engagingly modern deconstruc-tionist adrift in an infinity of texts is also, after all, the Richardson who complained that 'the press groans beneath infidelity, indecency, libel, faction, nonsense' because legal authority did not stand sentinel over it.[28] Richardson believed strongly in censorship, and as far as we can tell never printed a work of which he did not personally

27 This is history's majority verdict, not mine. Richardson seems to me pious and high-minded, nothing more.
28 Quoted by Eaves and Kimpel, *Samuel Richardson*, p. 435.

approve.[29] Having published *Clarissa*, he undertook in the next two editions a massive policing operation of his own text, overhauling its discourse to expunge infelicities and forestall misinterpretations. Indeed it is worth recalling in this respect the etymological link between *police* and *polite*. Throughout his life, Richardson constantly patrolled his works in the interests of 'polite letters', erasing solecisms, 'low' terms, mistakes of social manners and potential indelicacies,[30] anxiously approximating his occasionally horny-handed prose to the standards of gentility. As the most cited living author in Johnson's dictionary, it would seem that he largely succeeded. But his most vital revisions were not simply questions of etiquette. The chief purpose of this exhausting labour was to control the interpretations of his texts. Exasperated by perverse critics who found Lovelace attractive and Clarissa over-scrupulous, Richardson added to the novel a plethora of material designed to insulate it against such misprisions. The irony of this enterprise has already been suggested: the more Richardson plugs and patches to disambiguate his writing and avert incorrect readings, the more he piles on matter for yet further misconstruction. Driven on by what must surely be seen as a quasi-pathological urge for perfection, Richardson succeeds in unravelling his text a little more, prising it open in the act of trying to spring it shut. In striving to 'complete' his work, to achieve the utterly definitive text,

29 See William M. Sale Jr, *Samuel Richardson: Master Printer* (Ithaca NY, 1950), chapter 6 *passim*.
30 Not enough, however, to satisfy the octogenarian Charles Povey, who fulminates against the immorality of *Pamela* in his *The Virgin in Eden* (1742): 'Good God! Can amorous embraces delineated in these images, tend to inculcate religion in the minds of youth, when the blood is hot, and runs quick in every vein? Are these lights to direct the soul to a crucify'd Jesus?' (quoted by Eaves and Kimpel, *Samuel Richardson*, p. 131). Povey worked in fire insurance.

he simply sets himself more to do.[31]

Yet it would be a mistake to see this process as *merely* ironic. For Richardson does of course have some success in delimiting intentions and controlling his novels' reception, banishing egregious misreadings and blatantly pre-empting the hermeneutical act. And though the liberal critics naturally find this thought-policing distasteful, it is surely obvious how utterly integral it was to Richardson's project. For how could a devout eighteenth-century puritan permit licentious interpretations of his fiction? How could the reader conceivably be allowed to approve of a brutal rapist? Richardson was no Henry James, bland in the midst of ambiguities; he was a courageous spokesman for middle-class ideology, a properly didactic, propagandist writer. The historic interests he espoused were too urgent to be traded for the thrills of aesthetic ambivalence. If that later bourgeois Henry James could tolerate multiple interpretation, it was in part because strenuous ideologues like Richardson had been there before him, laying the social basis of that textual licence. Deeply ambiguous though Richardson's novels are, he would have found the modern liberal's complacent cult of confusion simply obnoxious. And though he preached a good many obnoxious doctrines himself, he would surely have been right. The delight Richardson took in hearing that one of his works had persuaded a reader to mend his dissolute ways can now only be thought naïve; 'art' is supposed to affect 'life', of course, but not in such embarrassingly direct ways.

31 A point well elaborated by William Beatty Warner in his *Reading Clarissa: The Struggles of Interpretation* (New Haven, 1979). Richardson himself was wryly aware of this problem: 'And I have run into such a length! — And am such a sorry pruner, though greatly luxuriant, that I am apt to add three pages for one I take away!' (*Selected Letters*, p. 61). For Richardson's revisions of *Clarissa*, see Mark Kinkead-Weekes, '*Clarissa* Restored?', *Review of English Studies* NS 10, 1959, and T. C. Duncan Eaves and Ben D. Kimpel, 'The Composition of *Clarissa* and its Revision before Publication', *PMLA* 83 (1), 1968.

Literature should not propagandize: instead it should forcefully persuade us that, say, personal relationships are the highest good, or that all propositions are relative. One can be sure that most of those who find Richardson's delight naïve would also find a drama which incited its audience of sweated labourers to strike incorrigibly vulgar.

Epic theatre, by virtue of its variable viewpoint, disowns one traditional device for securing ideological closure: the presence of a coherent overview or 'metalanguage' which may direct the audience's response. On the contrary, the 'closure' such theatre seeks to effect is nothing less than the militant viewpoint that all such metalanguages must be suspected. By using the epistolary form, Richardson equally deprives himself of this resource: you cannot have an authorial voice-over if the characters do all the writing. It is, indeed, just here that the main ideological dilemma of form in Richardson lies. For on the one hand, nothing could be more ideologically effective than writing 'to the moment', tracing the very ebb and recoil of experience as it happens, and thus admitting the privileged reader to the very sanctum of the spontaneously 'real'. Yet on the other hand, as Richardson complains,

> It is impossible that readers the most attentive, can always enter into the views of the writer of a piece written, as hoped, to Nature and the moment. A species of writing, too, that may be called new; and every one putting him and herself into the character they read, and judging of it by their own sensations.[32]

Richardson's own forms make him understandably nervous. As a sound empiricist, he resents the intrusion of an impersonal language between the reader and the real; the ideological affect must be borne straight to the consumer with a minimum of mediation:

32 *Selected Letters*, p. 316.

Such a sweetness of temper, so much patience and resignation, as she seems to be mistress of; yet writing of and in the midst of *present* distresses! How *much more* lively and affecting, for that reason, must her style be; her mind tortured by the pangs of uncertainty (the events then hidden in the womb of fate) *than* the dry, narrative, unanimated style of persons, relating difficulties and dangers surmounted; the relator perfectly at ease; and if himself unmoved by his own story, not likely greatly to affect the reader![33]

Literature, as we might now say, must be *discours* rather than *langue*, implicating rather than abolishing a speaking subject.[34] Yet the case contains a familiar empiricist flaw: if reading subject confronts literary object with no mediation but 'experience', and if experience is notoriously variable, how is it that there are not as many textual interpretations as there are readers? Perhaps there are; in which case the alarmed author must discover some means of allowing his readers to 'enter into the views of the writer', policing this dangerous dissemination of discourse, returning the prodigal text to its distraught father. It is this which spurs him to further writing – to appending, for example, a flagrantly tendentious 'table of contents' to *Clarissa*, a kind of menu that drops broad hints about which dishes are worth trying.

The author, then, must dominate his text even when it threatens to decentre him. Richardson is not above teasing his readers, deliberately fashioning debatable situations, artfully dispersing them among disparate

33 *Clarissa* (London, 1962), vol. 4, p. 81. Richardson quotes some of these words in his Introduction to the novel.
34 See Émile Benveniste, *Problèmes de linguistique générale* (Paris, 1966), p. 206f.

interpretations.[35] But for all the erotic sport of such textual teasings, the printer remains master, coyly leading his readers up the garden path only to regroup them submissively around him in the grotto. Richardson's relations with his circle of women, who would sit around him in the garden as he read from his works, is in this sense an exact image of his textual relations with his readers. That audience is not to be bullied into a univocal meaning: a degree of banter, dissent, free play is perfectly permissible. But this harmless eroticism coexists with a mild dash of sadism, as the author exults in prolonging his readers' suspense, slyly withholding a narrative outcome, manipulating their fears and affections. A 'bashful' and 'sheepish' creature in real life, Richardson confessed that 'In writing … I was always an impudent man.'[36] He would, no doubt,

---

35 '… in this sort of writing, something, as I have hinted should be left (to the reader) to make out or debate upon. The whole story abounds with situations and circumstances debatable. It is not an unartful management to interest the readers so much in the story, as to make them differ in opinion as to the capital articles, and by leading one, to espouse one, another, another, opinion, make them all, if not authors, carpers ….' (*Selected Letters*, p. 296)

36 *Selected Letters*, p. 319. Richardson's erotic teasing is nowhere better illustrated than in the extraordinary farce of his attempts to meet his admiring but then personally unknown correspondent Lady Bradshaigh in the flesh. Lady Bradshaigh, shy of meeting the great man after some 'impudent' critical comments in her letters to him, proposed that he should take a stroll in St James's Park, so that after a glimpse of him she might better decide whether she had the nerve to face him. Richardson duly took a turn in the park, fortified with a sea biscuit, but Lady Bradshaigh did not appear. A week later he paraded up and down Pall Mall for some time and was again disappointed. Some time later he tried to entice her into his house by the legendary gambit of mentioning a drawing of Clarissa (specially borrowed from a friend for the occasion) which she might like to see. This move also failed. By this time Richardson was becoming distinctly irritated, a fact he made plain in correspondence to Lady

have understood all but the last word of T. S. Eliot's wry remark about the *'braggadocio* of the mild-mannered man safely entrenched behind his typewriter'.[37] His writing would seem in part aggressive compensation for a sense of social inferiority, a virile dominance meekly defused in everyday life. It is no wonder that he detested *Tristram Shandy*, with its 'Unaccountable wildness; whimsical digressions; comical incoherencies; uncommon indecencies',[38] rattled as he must have been by a writing which constantly escalates beyond its author's control.[39] Literary licence and libidinal release, digressions and indecencies, are implicitly equated, as they are rather differently in his friend Elizabeth Carter's arch comment about the need to keep the pre-publication volumes of *Grandison* he had sent her out of the hands of other women. If she released Sir Charles to them, 'I apprehend there would be so much scratching & clawing that it would be impossible to keep him in my possession & he would run some hazard of

---

Bradshaigh, who then contritely walked in the park herself; this time it was his turn to stand her up. On a further occasion they passed each other four times in the park without meeting, though Lady Bradshaigh recognized Richardson by his description. Richardson, annoyed that her curiosity had been satisfied but not his, continued to stalk around the park in search of her, until physical exhaustion drove him back home. Lady Bradshaigh continued to fend off invitations to visit Richardson at his home, but finally agreed to see him at her own. This Richardson refused to do. The couple finally met on 6 March 1750.

37 *To Criticize the Critic* (London, 1978), p. 14.

38 *Selected Letters*, pp. 341–2.

39 It is, of course, possible to read this authorial impotence of Sterne's as merely a more devious form of bullying, a mildly sadistic teasing not far from Richardson's own. As a former student of mine, Tim Vaughan, once remarked, Sterne's bemused invitation to the reader to draw his own Widow Wadman might perhaps be better read: 'Draw your own bloody Widow Wadman.'

being scattered to the four winds of heaven.'[40] Grandison/ Richardson must be possessed as private sexual property lest he disseminate promiscuously among others; the text, imminently in danger of being fragmented, must be preserved whole and entire. 'I labour'd hard to rein in my invention,' remarks Richardson of *Pamela Part 2*, a strange self-plaudit for an artist.[41] He certainly succeeded. The indecent liberties of 'invention' must be suppressed in the cause of instruction, ideological closure achieved by a *calculated* sacrifice of *jouissance*.

Marooned between *langue* and *discours*, doctrine and experience, dominance and dissemination, Richardson's novels know a conflict between what Ian Watt has termed 'realism of presentation' and 'realism of assessment'.[42] On this theory, it takes the burgeoning English novel some time to reconcile showing with saying, dramatic action with moral commentary. By the time of Jane Austen, the novel has evolved beyond this probationary awkwardness into a mature synthesis of narrative realism and authorial evaluation. What is overlooked by this teleology of technique? Technically speaking, Richardson could no doubt have pulled off what Jane Austen did; but the ideological exigencies of his fiction demanded otherwise. If Richardson is not Jane Austen, it is partly because at his historical point certain richly effective forms of writing – moral homily, meditation, polemic, propaganda, exemplary tale – have not yet been relegated by a narrowing 'formal realism' to the scrapheap of literary sub-cultures. There is no reason why such discourses should not cohabit within the same covers, just because they are different. A. M. Kearney is right to detect a conflict in *Pamela* between two 'voices': the one 'spontaneous' and experiential, the

40 Quoted by Eaves and Kimpel, *Samuel Richardson*, p. 356.
41 *Selected Letters*, p. 54.
42 *The Rise of the Novel* (Harmondsworth, 1966), chapters 1 and 10.

other polite and sententious. It is just that he instinctively regards this as an aesthetic flaw: 'No one similarly situated, we are forced to admit,' he remarks of Pamela's more literary effusions, 'would express themselves thus.'[43] Why should we be *forced* to admit it? Nobody ever spoke like Lear either. Perhaps this is a flaw when it comes to 'realism'; but then what sort of 'realist' is Richardson? Nobody capable of perpetrating *Pamela Part 2* could possibly have regarded his realism in Austenite terms. 'The two voices,' comments Kearney, 'are never successfully fused'; Richardson allows his characters to speak spontaneously, but then 'intrud[es] as commentator regardless of dramatic context'. Exactly the same is true of epic theatre, where choruses perversely insist upon delivering commentaries apparently at odds with what has just happened. For epic theatre, the conflict between the two modes is, of course, precisely the point. Why *should* the two practices be 'fused'? What is the significance of their dislocation?

This, surely, is the question to be addressed to *Pamela*, a novel which it is today deeply perplexing to know how to read. As Kearney implies, it will not do to read it as 'formal realism'; it is not only too morally discursive for that, but also too fantastic. On the other hand it is clearly too realist to be read simply as symbolic wish-fulfilment or moral fable. It is even difficult to decide how funny it is meant to be. When are we allowed to laugh, if at all, and when does the text laugh with us? Perhaps the closest analogue to *Pamela* is a *double entendre* so blatantly libidinal that we cannot say whether it is joke, parapraxis or seriously meant. There are moments in literature — Jane Eyre's admiration for Rochester's long muscular arm, for example — which seem so flagrantly 'unconscious' in

43 'Richardson's *Pamela*: the Aesthetic Case', *Review of English Literature* 7, July 1966, p. 81.

import that we are almost instantly sure they are not. An 'innocent' reading is immediately followed by a sceptical one, only to be partly reinstated; suspended between the two readings, we wonder whether the text knows more or less than we do, and whether, if it knows what we know, we really know what we thought we knew. As good post-Freudian readers subtly vigilant to unconscious intentions, it seems possible that we have the laugh on *Pamela*; but on the other hand it may always have the laugh on us. Irwin Gopnik points out that relatively little of the sexual imagery of *Clarissa* is in fact 'unconscious' — indeed the characters sometimes discuss it quite openly.[44] For Hazlitt, Richardson is a good deal too conscious: 'Everything is too conscious in his works. Everything is distinctly brought home to the mind of his actors in the scene, which is a fault undoubtedly: but then it must be confessed, everything is brought home in its full force to the mind of the reader also.'[45] Richardson's novels certainly appear 'neurotic', bristling with tell-tale symptoms to be deciphered; but they can just as easily confront the analyst with the embarrassments of the psychotic whose unconscious does not need to be deciphered because it is all on the surface. Few English novels are so resonant of the repressed as Richardson's, and few before James so intricately self-conscious either, so full of finely articulate discourse and hair's-breadth discriminations. The reader has no sooner cynically suspected that Pamela may be a little schemer than Mr B. says it for us. Perhaps Pamela, as William Empson maintains, is *unconsciously* scheming;[46]

---

44 *A Theory of Style and Richardson's 'Clarissa'* (The Hague, 1970), p. 63.
45 'Lectures on the Comic Writers', p. 119.
46 'Tom Jones', *The Kenyon Review* 20, Spring 1958, p. 238. Leslie Fiedler adds an extra nuance by referring to Pamela's '*almost* unconscious duplicity' (*Love and Death in the American Novel*, p. 60).

but is the novel conscious of her unconscious or collusive with it? Do we laugh with Pamela at the novel's solemn moralizing of her 'baser' motives, or laugh with the novel at her slippery self-apologias? Do we have the edge over both novel and Pamela, or does the novel have the edge over us all? In inviting us to indulge our fantasies, is it cruder or cleverer than we are?

The two discrepant voices A. M. Kearney discerns in *Pamela* belong with these undecidabilities. But the ideological necessity of this disturbance still needs to be located. Richardson has available to him two forms of discourse to counter aristocratic insolence: the one a polite, highly formalized language of bourgeois—genteel morality which he contributes to shaping; the other the colloquial speech of the petty bourgeoisie. The latter is the idiom which stirs Clara Thompson to disdain Pamela as 'a vulgar, practical little soul',[47] a shrewd, racy speech of knowingness and spite, a perky blending of salt and sauce. Eaves and Kimpel point out how innovative Richardson was to place such language near the centre of his fiction, in contrast, say, to the 'comparatively colourless English' of a Moll Flanders.[48] Yet it was clearly not a discourse with history on its side: as Richardson revised his text he rubbed it steadily away, without eradicating it altogether. This was not the tongue in which aristocracy and bourgeoisie were to conclude their ideological pact; it was not to be heard so plainly again in English fiction until the early Dickens. *Pamela Part 1*, as Margaret Doody has suggested in her valuable account,[49] is at one level a genuinely *popular* novel: a text of the 'people', farcical

47 *Samuel Richardson: A Biographical and Critical Study* (London, 1900), p. 156.
48 *Samuel Richardson*, p. 109.
49 *A Natural Passion: A Study of the Novels of Samuel Richardson* (Oxford, 1974).

and festive, with strains of a comedy and 'naturalness' to be gradually expunged (not least by Richardson himself) from polite letters. But this idiom is constantly imbricated with anonymous, 'juridical' writing, which in the end will all but submerge it. The fissuring of 'formal realism' in *Pamela* is determined, in part, by an historical conflict between two essential yet disparate styles: the emergent metalanguage of bourgeois morality, and a still resilient popular speech.

It is, to some extent, a conflict between public discourse and private reflection. '"Thou knowest nothing, wench," said [Lady Davers], "of what belongs to people of condition; how should'st thou?" — "Nor," thought I, "do I desire it at this rate." "What shall I say, Madam?" said I...'[50] Pamela often enough suppresses a tart remark in the name of decorum, and this hiatus between social intercourse and 'interior speech'[51] is already a sort of structural guilt. Even the frankest characters in fiction seem a little two-faced once we have access to the thoughts they diplomatically suppress; and even where those subversive thoughts go unreported, as with the later 'exalted' Pamela, we cannot avoid the unworthy suspicion that they are still lurking somewhere. Committing your private thoughts to paper is itself a guilty act in Richardson. Pamela is relieved when the repentant Mr B., admitted to the last favour of reading her private journal, uncovering her text, finds nothing there at odds with public decorum — finds, as it were, an unbroken membrane. It is untrue that Pamela, in Mr B.'s emotionally blackmailing taunts, is a 'saucebox' and 'hypocrite', but neither is it true that she is exactly 'innocent'. The woman's very need to look sharp for sexual predators entails an obsession with virginity at

50 *Pamela*, vol. 1, p. 358.
51 See V. N. Vološinov, *Marxism and the Philosophy of Language* (New York and London, 1973), pp. 28–9, 37–9.

once necessary and compromising. The pre-marital Pamela is an engagingly realistic woman, shrewd, practical and humorous, and it is precisely this which makes her absolutism about sexuality seem so contrived. But if Pamela and the novel indeed fetishize sexuality, 'specializing a general crisis to a personal and (in its context) fashionable issue',[52] what tactic after all could be more soberly realist in a society ruled by Mr Bs? The contradiction of patriarchy is that Pamela is forced to treat herself as a sexual object in order to avoid becoming one for others; and the social necessity of such reification has to be taken along with what Raymond Williams calls its 'isolating fanaticism'. Pamela is indeed a 'vulgar, practical little soul', admirably adroit and resourceful; but this merely serves to foreground the 'unnaturalness' of a social order which drives women to cherish lofty thoughts about the 'jewel' of their 'virtue'. Her 'pertness', as she is well aware, is a vital mode of self-affirmation, a rupturing of polite discourse to avoid a worse violation. 'This, I suppose, makes me such a sauce-box, and bold-face, and a creature; and all because I won't be a sauce-box and bold-face indeed.'[53] The absolutist codes of puritan morality are in one sense comically at odds with practical petty-bourgeois experience, the novel's 'theoretical' and 'practical' ideologies farcically discrepant.[54] But in another sense those humourless pieties and literary disquisitions are the only defence of the weak: nothing short of a whole moral metalanguage is likely to avert the assaults of a B. How 'bold' or 'devious' Pamela is is finally undecidable, for what counts as cheek in the defence of your sexual integrity? Pamela is neither 'naturally' saucy nor a straitlaced girl driven desperately to impudence;

52 Raymond Williams, *The Country and the City* (London, 1973), p. 65.
53 vol. 1, p. 57.
54 See Louis Althusser, *For Marx* (London, 1969), p. 13.

she is neither deliberately scheming nor in the least blind to self-interest, neither initially high-minded nor a hypocrite. If we hesitate between these textual options, it is because of the material contradiction that at once de-sexualizes and over-sexualizes women.

There is a further sense in which the simple oppositions of 'innocence' and 'guilt' are partly deconstructed in Pamela. Pamela is both realist character and bearer of Richardson's ideological project of integration with the gentry; so it is not her fault, so to speak, if she is sometimes forced by those textual exigencies to act suspiciously. If she faints or fails to escape at convenient moments, it is because she is, as Mr B. himself heavily hints, part of a comic romance, whose social logic must not be imperilled by her complete plausibility. Pamela's 'guilt' is that she is no free agent but the function of an historical *plot* which the bourgeoisie have been long hatching. Her 'unconscious' − the implausible slips and enigmas of her behaviour − is the working in the text of this highly self-conscious strategy. *Pamela*'s 'unconscious' is in this sense the by-product of its conscious ends, the psychoanalytic shadow cast by its clear-eyed politics. Ambiguity is an essential lubricant of the ideological machine, at once 'residue' and structural necessity. If the reader is to be in full possession of the work's motives, it is vital that Pamela should not be in full possession of her own. And yet what reader could 'fully possess' this most brazenly fantastic of texts, which achieves its ideological ends in part by formal preaching, in part by the most shameless manipulations of our unconscious wish-fulfilment? One would be bold indeed to unravel what was 'conscious' and what 'unconscious' in a work whose unconscious engages the reader's in the cause of a conscious project of which Pamela's unconscious is one effect.

From a realist viewpoint, nothing could be more damaging to Pamela's credibility than the flatulent compliments

to her virtue she blandly reports. But Richardson, once
more, is not a James, concerned to enthrone some 'air
of reality' as an end in itself. There is no reason to sacrifice
the novel's didactic force to Pamela's proper modesty. Or,
for that matter, to Mark Kinkead-Weekes's complaint that
Mr B. is so 'externally' presented.[55] For a liberal realist
like Kinkead-Weekes, such 'externality' is automatically
defective: couldn't Richardson have surrendered B. a bit
more of the script, imaginatively dramatized his 'point of
view'? Perhaps *Galileo* would have benefited if Brecht had
allowed us a glimpse of the Grand Inquisitor's heart. As a
puritan ideologue, however, Richardson has no need to
make Mr B. more than a properly two-dimensional plot-
function, a straightforward class stereotype; we are not
asked to 'experience' his ridiculous spiritual conversion,
merely to register its point. 'Imaginative sympathy', that
talisman of liberal–realist criticism, is for Richardson one
mode of writing among several; it has no unquestioned
monopoly. By the end of *Pamela Part 1*, *discours* has
yielded ground to *langue*: Pamela the pert colloquialist has
become Pamela the genteel housewife, tirelessly producing
anonymous platitudes. Her linguistic absorption into the
ruling class is effectively complete, to be drearily per-
petuated in *Pamela Part 2*. But what makes much of
Pamela boring and repugnant is Richardson's ideological
values, not his forms. There is no reason in principle why
didacticism and propaganda should not be more moving
than dramatic realism. It is not the metalanguage which is
objectionable, just what Richardson says in it. When Mr B.
promulgates his scrupulously codified opinions as to what
makes a dutiful wife, Pamela is allowed a few last shreds
of 'inner speech', a flicker or two of ironic reservations;
but it is the merest gesture. She is now the collusive victim
of patriarchy, triumphantly elevated into enemy territory.

55 Introduction to *Pamela*, p. xi.

Reading these painful passages, it is difficult to imagine how *Pamela* could in any sense be proclaimed as 'progressive'. The same question could be asked of women's romances today: are they anything more than opiate and offensive? In both cases, surely, the answer is guardedly positive. *Pamela* tells the story of a woman snatched into the ruling class and tamed to its sexist disciplines; yet it contains, grotesque though it may sound, a utopian element. The novel is a kind of fairy-tale pre-run of *Clarissa*, a fantasy wish fulfilment in which abduction and imprisonment turn out miraculously well, the rough beast becomes a prince charming and the poor kitchen maid a beautiful princess. It is, so to speak, a cartoon version of *Clarissa*, simplified, stereotyped and comic in outcome. Like modern romantic fiction, its main effect is thus anodyne and oppressive — a cynical displacement of women's sufferings into consolatory myth, a false, insulting 'resolution' of sexual combat which merely consolidates patriarchal power. Yet one of the most striking aspects of such degraded fiction in our own time is the demand for it: the depressing truth that it does, in however monstrously debased a form, express an implicit dissatisfaction with current social conditions.[56] However subjectively reactionary such fables may be, they signify an objective hiatus between desire and the real, a diseased impulse to transcendence. *Pamela* is a sickly celebration of male ruling-class power; but it is also a fierce polemic against the prejudice that the most inconspicuous serving maid cannot be as humanly valuable as her social superiors. The turgid idealizing of its heroine is both mystification and critique: it flatters the absorptive powers of patriarchy at

---

56 For a valuable study of popular romances in their ideological context, see Helga Geyer-Ryan, 'Der andere Roman. Versuch über die verdrängte Ästhetik des Populären' (unpublished Ph.D. thesis, Free University of Berlin, 1981), especially chapter 4.

the same time as it questions its class bias. Richardson, indeed, was worried that his novel had gone too far: would it encourage every gentleman in the realm to marry his maid?[57] Anxious to forestall such 'levelling' interpretations, Richardson insisted that Pamela was an extraordinary case: it was her unusual goodness which made her so meritorious. If he thus buttressed the class structure he so profoundly respected, he also stressed the individuality of the woman Pamela in a way alien to our own depersonalizing romances, for which any woman may be indifferently rescued from slavery to success. A similar indifference was apparent in Samuel Johnson, for whom individuality was dispensable when it came to marriage; he believed the whole process should be nationalized, organized by the Lord Chancellor.[58] If this view was already outmoded in the late eighteenth century, it was due in some measure to Richardson's defence of that partly enslaving, partly emancipatory ideology, romantic love.

The gap between public speech and mental reservation, metalanguage and salty colloquialism, is, I have argued, closed by the end of *Pamela Part 1*. By the time of *Part 2*, Sir Simon Darnford is complaining that Pamela has banished the *double entendre* ('the salt, the sauce' of discourse) from the surrounding countryside.[59] That closure consummates a project begun with Richardson's two early works, *The Apprentice's Vade Mecum* and the *Familiar Letters*: the task of regulating forms of discourse for the petty bourgeoisie and working classes, instructing them in the discursive rules of polite society. The stage is then set for the entry of Clarissa, a character whose very inner speech is impeccably genteel, whose most

57   Henry Fielding, author of the satirical *Shamela*, did just that.
58   See Lawrence Stone, *The Family, Sex and Marriage in England*, p 129.
59   vol. 2, p. 72.

confessional outpourings rarely swerve from textbook orthodoxy. Racy colloquialism in that novel is relegated to the villainous aristocrat, an irresponsible speech which must be stemmed. Yet just as this whole enterprise grows to fruition in *Clarissa*, it is very nearly sunk without trace. Having patiently perfected the language of class collaboration, Richardson then produces a novel which all but tears that text down the middle. The pact between bourgeoisie and nobility has been achieved in form; it is now about to be shattered in content.[60] *Pamela* represents the comic moment of an aspiring class, buoyant, affirmative and, like all cartoons, magically insulated from grave injury. But if Richardson is a bourgeois ideologue in his obsession with contracts and regulations, he is equally so in his commitment to individual freedom, and the two will prove incompatible. In a devastating demystification, *Clarissa* will give us the tragic reality.

60 This is one reason why Mark Kinkead-Weekes's essentially teleological reading of the movement from *Pamela* to *Clarissa* will not do. (See his Introduction to *Pamela*, p. xii.)

The Rape of Clarissa

'*Good God!*,' writes Lovelace to Clarissa Harlowe, 'What is *now* to become of me! How shall I support this disappointment! No new cause! On one knee, kneeling with the other, I write! My feet benumbed with midnight wanderings through the heaviest dews that ever fell: my wig and my linen dripping with the hoar frost dissolving on them!'[1]

Richardson does not, presumably, intend this kind of thing to be funny. To confess the humour of the wet-wigged Lovelace scribbling an exasperated note on his frozen knee would be to strike at the root of the Richardsonian ideology of writing: the fiction that 'experience' can be conveyed in all its living immediacy by language, the faith that writing and reality may be at one. Richardson saw that he had invented a new species of writing, a set of 'instantaneous descriptions and reflections' which were 'to the moment';[2] but it might equally be called a kind of anti-writing, one which strives to abolish the materiality of the sign, its treacherous power to divide and displace meaning, by reducing it to the humble receptable of the 'real'. The master printer will indeed struggle throughout his writing to master print, wrenching it into the unambiguous

1 *Clarissa*, Everyman edition (London, 1978), vol. 1, p. 327.
2 Author's Preface to *Clarissa*, vol. 1, p. xiv, and *Selected Letters*, p. 316.

service of his message, permitting no troubling gap to open between 'experience' and 'expression'.

It is this ideology of representation which characterizes Clarissa herself.[3] 'I always speak and write the sincere dictates of my heart,'[4] she tells her friend Anna Howe, appealing to the purity of authorial intention against the duplicities of interpretation: 'But of this I assure you, that whatever interpretation my words were capable of, I *intended not* any reserve to you. I wrote my heart, at the time....'[5] Anna herself is a less naïve semiotician, submitting Clarissa's writing to a 'symptomatic' reading, sardonically detecting in its bland denials and cautious proprieties the flickers of unconscious desire. Anna directs her deconstructive scepticism

> not...upon those passages which are written, though perhaps not *intended*, with such explicitness (don't be alarmed, my dear!) as leaves little cause of doubt: but only when you affect reserve; when you give new words for common things; when you come with your *curiosities*, with your *conditional likings*, and with your PRUDE-encies (mind how I spell the word) in a case, that with every other person defies all prudence — overt acts of treason all these, against the sovereign friendship we have vowed to each other![6]

Even Clarissa herself is pulled up from time to time by what Marx called the 'miracle-working power of the pen',

---

3 An ideology of the sign by now well enough interrogated in the works of Jacques Derrida. See in particular *Of Grammatology* (Baltimore and London, 1976).

4 vol. 1, p. 286. See also my own comments on writing and the eighteenth century in *Walter Benjamin, or Towards a Revolutionary Criticism*, pp. 14—19.

5 vol. 1, p. 190.

6 vol. 1, p. 188.

its capacity to exceed and invert her precise meaning: 'But whither roves my pen? How dare a perverse girl take these liberties with relations so very respectable, and whom she highly respects?'[7] 'Truth is truth, my dear!' Anna once reminds Clarissa;[8] but though the novel certainly trusts in this profound tautology, it cannot help noticing, being after all a novel, that such self-identity is ceaselessly disrupted by the practice of writing itself — indeed, that once taken literally, it would bring all writing to an abrupt end.

To qualify as a legitimate pursuit, writing must confine itself to the transparent communication of morally useful meaning. Yet even Clarissa is forced guiltily to concede that writing is also obsessive and excessive, compulsion and self-delight:

> And indeed, my dear, I know not how to *forebear* writing. I have now no other employment or diversion. And I must write on, although I were not to send it to anybody. You have often heard me own the advantages I have found from writing down everything of moment that befalls me; and of all I *think*, and of all I *do*, that may be of future use to me; for besides that this helps to form one to a style, and opens and expands the ductile mind, every one will find that many a good thought evaporates in thinking; many a good resolution goes off, driven out of memory perhaps by some other not so good. But when I set down what I *will* do, or what I *have* done, on this or that occasion, the resolution or action is before me either to be adhered to, withdrawn, or amended; and I have entered into *compact* with myself, as I may say; having given it under my own hand to *improve*, rather than to go *backward*, as I live longer.

7 vol. 1, p. 61.
8 vol. 2, p. 132.

I would willingly therefore write to *you* if I *might*; the rather as it would be more inspiriting to have some end in view in what I write, some friend to please, besides merely seeking to gratify my passion for scribbling.[9]

Writing as communication threatens to become a mere pretext for writing as invention, the sober end sheer occasion for the self-gratifying means; the puritan *écrivant* conceals a furtive *écrivain*, for whom script is sportive rather than instrumental.[10] Writing must officially have a point, as self-exhortation or moral *aide-mémoire*; even where it is self-communion, and so prone to the dangers of narcissism, it must mime a public 'compact', provide a mirror before which the author may unite with an 'ideal ego'. Officially, writing is a mere supplement to physical presence: 'Indeed I have no delight,' Clarissa tells Anna, '... equal to that which I take in conversing with you — by *letter* when I cannot in *person*.'[11] In his own correspondence, however, Richardson seems tempted to install the 'supplement' in place of the dissatisfying 'real':

This correspondence is, indeed, the cement of friend-ship: it is friendship avowed under hand and seal: friendship upon bond, as I may say: more pure, yet more ardent, and less broken in upon, than personal conversation can be even amongst the most pure, because of the deliberation it allows, from the very preparation to, and action of writing.... Who then shall decline the converse of the pen? The pen that makes distance, presence; and brings back to sweet remembrance all the delights of presence; which

9　vol. 2, p. 128.
10　See Roland Barthes, *Writing Degree Zero* (London, 1967).
11　vol. 1, p. 20.

makes even presence but body, while absence becomes the soul; and leaves no room for the intrusion of breakfast-calls, or dinner or supper direction, which often broke in upon us.[12]

Writing, in a curious paradox, is so graphically representational that it may dispense with what it denotes; pressed to its limit, such dogged representationalism capsizes into a sheer autonomy of script, for which the 'real' is body only in the sense of corpse. Only the death of the referent will release the soul of its meaning. For Richardson, 'absence becomes the soul' of writing in two opposed senses: on the one hand, as we shall see, writing perpetually stands in for a reality it can never encompass; on the other hand, less gloomily, the soul of the real is fleshed into full presence only by the withdrawal of the trivially physical. The intrusions of the material world, in which discourse is dispersed and refracted, yield to an unblemished plenitude of sense, an unfractured mutuality of subjects which is also a form of mastery. For writing permits re-writing: in the privacy of the boudoir you can control and recuperate meaning, as you cannot so easily in the irregular give-and-take of personal conversation. If Richardson is in one sense Cartesian, viewing writing as the soul or essence of a contingent material world, he is also contradictorily empiricist, seeing it as the mere supplement of experience. For all the ardent immediacy of the letter, for all the traces of the body inscribed on it (letters in Richardson come creased with rage or haste, blotted with sweat or tears), the one contract unattainable in correspondence is the sexual union of bodies. This, which is what all the letters of *Clarissa* are ultimately *about*, must also be what is palpably absent from them. Richardson sees well enough that sexuality is mainly a matter of discourse: the sexual power

12 *Selected Letters*, p. 65.

struggle between Clarissa and Lovelace is a primarily rhetorical affair, a matter of strategic textual moves, the gaining of a momentary linguistic advantage, the reluctant concession of a meaning. Yet this great flurry of signifying presence, the very soul of the real, merely foregrounds a material lack: letters can be no more than 'supplementary' sexual intercourse, eternally standing in for the real thing. Letters concede yet withhold physical intimacy in a kind of artfully prolonged teasing, a courtship which is never consummated; like Derrida's 'hymen', they join and divide at a stroke.[13] Richardson's representationalism is ironically incoherent: if writing is in one sense mere addition to reality, it is also the essence of an inert physical world which has become supplementary to it. If the sign is the death of the thing, that death is nevertheless redemptive: through its troubling blankness the body is resurrected into a presence more radiantly authentic than the unrisen flesh.

Released from the bondage of the body, writing is free to *master* it. If it embodies the heart's spontaneous stirrings it does so craftily, calculatingly, allowing a 'deliberation' alien to the conversing voice. The very soul of Nature, writing is also the most flagrant artifice, as strategic as it is spontaneous;[14] and the mystery is then how writing can at once mirror and manipulate experience, serve and rule it simultaneously. Writing must loyally reflect its object, interposing none of its own bulk between that and the

13 See *La Dissémination* (Paris, 1972), pp. 237f.
14 A point recognised by Samuel Johnson, who believed that the 'soul lies naked' in correspondence, but also held that 'There is ... no transaction which offers stronger temptations to fallacy and sophistication than epistolary intercourse.' ('Pope', *Lives of the Poets* (London, 1961), vol. 2, p. 298) William J. Farrell points out that Lovelace is being insincere when he speaks plainly and sincere when he is rhetorical ('Style and Action in *Clarissa*', *Studies in English Literature* 3 (3), 1963).

empathetic reader; but to influence the reader effectively it must also transcend its object, censoring and organizing it for public consumption. The problem of writing is in this sense the problem of the woman: how is she to be at once decorous and spontaneous, translucently candid yet subdued to social pressure? Writing, like women, marks a frontier between public and private, at once agonized outpouring and prudent strategem.[15]

'Strategem' is a Lovelace term; for if Clarissa's aesthetic is dourly representational, Lovelace's is one of reckless device. He is a post-structuralist precursor, master of neologism and (as with his dying words) *double entendre*, given to transcribing grunts and yawns semiotically, mildly radical in politics and fascinated by textual marginalia. ('I have often thought that the little words in the republic of letters, like the little folks in a nation, are the most significant.')[16] At times, as in his poker-faced proposal to pass his old age in morally instructing the young, the irony or seriousness of his discourse is simply undecidable. What is worrying about Lovelace in the early part of the novel is not so much that he preys upon women but that for a man he spends too much time writing. Whereas the repulsive bourgeois Solmes is barely literate, the cavalier Lovelace is 'a great plotter, and a great writer',[17] a pathological spinner of groundless narratives who 'has always a pen in his fingers when he retires'.[18] (There is no need to summon Freud here: the sexual innuendo, as often in Richardson, is surely self-conscious.) Lovelace's writing sparkles with sheer self-indulgent

15 See Ruth Perry, *Women, Letters and the Novel* (New York, 1980), for a useful discussion coupling the epistolary form and the condition of women in the eighteenth century.
16 vol. 2, p. 435.
17 vol. 1, p. 17.
18 vol. 1, p. 49.

jouissance, onanistic rather than copulatory, sign of the social unconstraint of the aristocrat who has 'a great portion of time upon his hands, to employ in writing, or worse'.[19] The suggestion that such promiscuous writing is radically dangerous is well justified: it is by persuading Clarissa to 'correspond privately' with him that Lovelace ensnares her in the first place, and as a full-blooded formalist he perceives that the mere event of correspondence outweighs the 'innocence' of its content. ('I know he has nothing to boast of from *what* you have written; but is not his inducing you to receive his letters, and to answer them, a great point gained?')[20] Lovelace begins by exploiting Clarissa's passion for scribbling rather than sexual affections, but the two impulses are intimately allied.

He himself sophistically denies that writing involves sexuality, in an intriguing parody of Richardson's own celebration of correspondence:

> I proceeded, therefore — That I loved familiar letter-writing, as I had more than once told her, above all the species of writing: it was writing from the heart (without the fetters prescribed by method or study), as the very word *correspondence* implied. Not the heart only; the *soul* was in it. Nothing of body, when friend writes to friend; the mind impelling sovereignly the vassal-fingers. It was, in short, friendship recorded; friendship given under hand and seal; demonstrating that the parties were under no apprehension of changing from time or accident, when they so liberally gave testimonies, which would always be ready, on failure or infidelity, to be turned against them.[21]

19   vol. 1, p. 51.
20   vol. 1, p. 45.
21   vol. 2, p. 431.

'Nothing of body': if this is unintentionally ironic (for Lovelace's whole aim in writing is of course to possess Clarissa's body), it is also self-undoing, for it shows how language does indeed have a 'body', a material weight of connotations, which outstrips authorial meaning. If it is meant as ironic it is equally self-undoing, for as we shall see Clarissa's body is indeed a sort of 'nothing', a sheer resistance to symbolization which signals the death of script. That the body finally escapes language is the subversive truth which this most remorselessly representational of texts will have finally to confront. 'Nothing of body': blandly desexualized, writing cuts free from the carnal only the more ably to wield dominance over it: 'the mind impelling sovereignly the vassal-fingers', male *écriture* subduing the female flesh to its pleasures. If 'body' means substance, law, constraint, there must indeed be none of it in the scriptive congress between the pair; such bodily resistance must be dissolved into the free play of the letter, so that Lovelace may finally come to inscribe Clarissa with his penis rather than his pen. Correspondence is private gratification, acknowledging no law beyond the mutual bearing of hearts or bodies. It is for this reason that Clarissa's suppression of *écriture* is a necessary protection of her sexual integrity. For writing, as Lovelace goes on to imply, does indeed possess a body, a thick and violent material being: it is a matter of record and contract, seal and bond, tangible documentation which may be turned against its author, cited out of context, deployed as threat, testimony, blackmail. It is the 'iterability' of script — the fact that its materiality allows it to be reproduced in changed conditions — which makes it such an efficient instrument of oppression. The free utterances of the heart, once taken down in writing, may always be used later in evidence against the speaker. Lovelace's own heartfelt celebration of writerly communion with Clarissa is, of course, craftily designed to contain precisely such a minatory sub-text within it. In treating her own writing as moral *aide-mémoire*, Clarissa lives an 'imaginary' relationship with herself within which such writing is always recuperable.[22] But this 'innocent' doubleness becomes under Lovelace's pen a perversion of the text against its author, shackling her with her own signs. Writing partakes of the body's permanence but shares the fluidity of the soul, and it is precisely in this Cartesian coupling that it is most potent: the utterance of the moment, once paralysed to print, is then secured for the most devious interpretative uses. If Lovelace can cite Clarissa's writing against her, his friend Belford can do just the same to him: 'Yet I know,' Lovelace writes to Belford, 'I am still furnishing thee with new weapons against myself.'[23]

The letter in *Clarissa*, then, is the site of a constant power struggle. For Clarissa herself, writing, like sexuality, is a private, always violable space, a secret enterprise fraught with deadly risk. In an oppressive society, writing is the sole free self-disclosure available to women, but it is precisely this which threatens to surrender them into that society's power. The Harlowes wrest writing materials from Clarissa in what she explicitly terms an 'act of violence',[24]

22 Cynthia Griffin Wolff relates this to the puritan impulse to preserve a detailed spiritual record, and discusses the role of the letter in sustaining a threatened identity. (See *Samuel Richardson and the Eighteenth Century Puritan Character* (New York, 1972).)

23 vol. 3, p. 204.

24 vol. 1, p. 402. R. Baird Shuman actually reads Richardson's first two novels as allegories of a conflict between the 'free' writer and the Licensing Act of 1737. Unfortunately for his argument, Richardson actually supported censorship, a fact not available to Shuman at the time of writing; but if 'licence' and 'censorship' are taken in a broader sense, Shuman's case that this is what *Pamela* and *Clarissa* are 'about' is not half as eccentric as it seems. (See 'Censorship as a Controlling Theme in *Pamela* and *Clarissa*', *Notes and Queries* NS 3, 1956.)

and Anna Howe rails similarly against maternal censorship. Letters, the most intimate sign of the subject, are waylaid, forged, stolen, lost, copied, cited, censored, parodied, misread, rewritten, submitted to mocking commentary, woven into other texts which alter their meaning, exploited for ends unforeseen by their authors. Writing and reading are always in some sense illicit intercourse — not only because they may be expressly forbidden, but because there is always the possibility of a fatal slip between intention and interpretation, emission and reception. As one letter spawns another, in that astonishing spasm of textual productivity which is *Clarissa*, the chances of such hermeneutical abuse multiply, the impulse to protect and control writing grows accordingly sharper, and more exploitable signs ironically result. Mrs Harlowe prefers her daughter to read rather than write — to conform herself to another's text rather than to produce her own meanings.

If letter-writing is in one sense free subjectivity, it is also the function of an ineluctable power system. Certainly no activity could be more minutely regulated. To 'correspond' is to implicate a set of political questions: Who may write to whom, under what conditions? Which parts may be cited to another, and which must be suppressed? Who has the authority to edit, censor, mediate, commentate? 'I charge you,' writes Mrs Harlowe to Clarissa, 'let not this letter be found. Burn it. There is too much of the *mother* in it to a daughter so unaccountably obstinate.'[25] If Lovelace's missives are without body, Mrs Harlowe's, apparently, have too much. But this regulation of writing is not just an external policing, a cumbersome apparatus stifling 'free expression'. It is part of propriety that the rules of acceptable discourse should be internalized, as spontaneous inner constraints on what one may legitimately say. Power is less the brutal inhibiting of truth

25   vol. 1, p. 119.

than its enabling condition. It is not only the arbitrary abrogation of writing but the internal censorship of decorum: what it is proper, and so possible, to *think*. It is by virtue of the rules governing polite discourse, not in spite of them, that Clarissa sustains her 'free' identity. Without such scrupulous divisions of the permissible from the unthinkable, she would have no positive being what-soever. Only by dint of such exact articulations is she able to articulate at all. This is not to claim that she is not 'repressed'; it is simply that such repression cannot be romantically conceived, as a rich inner life despotically denied public speech. Clarissa is precisely not a Jane Eyre. Her repression must rather be seen in Freudian terms, as those bodily impulses which have failed to achieve repre-sentation at all, severed as they are from inward as well as social discourse. Her mysterious self-identity, scandalous to the protean Lovelace, lies in the continuity between inner and public speech for which she strives. If Lovelace writes as he speaks, in the blasé jolts and jottings of his 'lively *present-tense* manner',[26] Clarissa speaks as she writes, as admirably undishevelled in oral style as she is in her script. It is not exactly that her writing reflects her experience but that her experience is, as it were, already 'written', decorously conformed to allowable dis-course, imprinted by the web of power relations to which she 'freely' submits. There are indeed, as we have seen, 'symptomatic' flaws in her writing, evasions and ambigui-ties which fissure her self-possession; but this is not a matter of some turbulent 'inner speech' restlessly at odds with script.

The letter in *Clarissa* is double-edged: it is private confidence and political weapon, intimacy and intrigue, a jealously protected space in which you never cease to be publicly at stake. In Mikhail Bakhtin's term, it is *dialogic*

26   vol. 3, p. 195.

language.[27] In the very heart of anguish or confession, the letter can never forget that it is turned outwards to another, that its discourse is ineradicably social. Such sociality is not just contingent, a mere matter of its destination; it is the very material condition of its existence. The other to whom the letter is addressed is included within it, an absent recipient present within each phrase. As speech-for-another, the letter must reckon that recipient's likely response into its every gesture. In a pleasing anticipation of modern reception theory, the dying Clarissa requests her mother to 'fill up chasms' in her disjointed text.[28] The letter is the sign doubled, overhearing itself in the ears of its addressee; and in this sense 'public' and 'private' are inseparably interwoven within it. But such doubleness also opens the permanent risk of duplicity. For if subject and society are in one sense mutually imbricated, they are also in potential contradiction: you must write with a wary eye on the other, who may confiscate or abuse your most secret reflections. 'Natural' as it is, the letter is therefore also a guilty artifice: in an individualist society, nothing could be at once more permissible, and more perilous, than communicating your private thoughts to others.

The paradox of *Clarissa* is that Clarissa's writing is 'masculine' whereas Lovelace's is 'feminine'. It has been claimed that men and women under patriarchy relate differently to the act of writing. Men, more deeply marked by the 'transcendental signifier' of the phallus, will tend to view signs as stable and whole, ideal entities external to the body; women will tend to live a more inward, bodily relationship to script.[29] Whatever the dangers of such

27   See his *Problems of Dostoevsky's Poetics* (Ann Arbor, 1973).
28   vol. 4, p. 302.
29   See Luce Irigaray, *Ce sexe qui n'en est pas un* (Paris, 1977), and Michèle Montrelay, *L'ombre et le nom* (Paris, 1977).

stereotyping notions, nothing could be more appropriate to *Clarissa*. Clarissa herself exerts the fullest possible control over her meanings, sustaining an enviable coherence of sense even through her worst trials: 'You will find the sense surprisingly entire, her weakness considered,' remarks Belford of one of her dying letters.[30] Lovelace's writing is mercurial, diffuse, exuberant. Clarissa's letters are signs of a unified self, orderly regimes of sense that brook no contradiction. Behind them stands a transcendental subject, apparently unscathed by her own slips and evasions, whose relationship to writing is dominative and instrumental. Lovelace, by contrast, lives on the interior of his prose, generating a provisional identity from the folds of his text, luxuriating in multiple modes of being. He is happy to be 'written' by his own autonomous plots: 'Such a joy when any roguery is going forward! – I so little its master!'[31] Both styles of script are in some sense narcissistic; but whereas Clarissa's narcissism resembles that of the Lacanian 'mirror stage',[32] in which letters reflect back to their author an image of idealized self-unity, Lovelace's has the more polymorphous quality of auto-eroticism. His writing is less the mirror of the self than the very stage on which it plays out its self-delighting metamorphoses. So sharp a contrast naturally requires modification. We have seen already that Clarissa is by no means as coherent a subject as she would wish herself – that her sober ideology of the sign cannot altogether banish the covert pleasures of *écriture*. Lovelace, conversely, scorns any vulgar *end* of writing, comically aware that the energy he devotes to seducing Clarissa is ludicrously disproportionate to its goal; yet his letters are, after all, cruelly instrumental to that purpose, and their

30 vol. 4, p. 329.
31 vol. 2, p. 186.
32 See Jacques Lacan, 'The Mirror Stage', *Écrits* (London, 1977).

cavalier sportiveness powered by a pathological compulsion: 'I must write on, and cannot help it.'[33] It is because
such an obsession, as we shall see, can never know an end
that its appropriate form is the self-generating letter; but
for all their gratuitous aestheticism, such letters are nevertheless weapons in the end-game of rape.

There is no question, then, of any simple opposition
between masculine and feminine, 'work' and 'text',[34] the
possessed and protean self. The letter in *Clarissa* is masculine and feminine together. I have suggested that it lies on
some troubled frontier between private and public worlds,
symbol at once of the self and of its violent appropriation.
Nothing could be at once more intimate and more alien-
able, flushed with the desire of the subject yet always ripe
for distortion and dishonour. In this sense, the letter
comes to signify nothing quite so much as female sexuality
itself, that folded, secret place which is always open to
violent intrusion. The sex/text metaphor in Richardson is
so insistent that it is difficult to believe it unconscious.
The male's desire to view the female's letters is shamelessly
voyeuristic: Pamela wears her text around her waist, Mr B.
threatens to strip her to discover it, and Lovelace swears
that 'I shall never rest until I have discovered where the
dear creature puts her letters.'[35] There is always within
the letter's decorously covered body that crevice or
fissured place where the stirrings of desire can be felt, that
slippage of meaning within which another may brutally
inscribe himself. The letter is that part of the body which
is detachable: torn from the very depths of the subject, it
can equally be torn from her physical possession, opened
by meddling fingers, triumphantly blazoned across a

33   vol. 2, p. 498.
34   See Roland Barthes, 'From Work to Text', *Image—Music—Text*
(London, 1977).
35   vol. 3, p. 52.

master-text, hijacked as trophy or stashed away as spoils.

In a well-known essay, Freud speaks of the 'detachable' parts of the human body, those hybrid, problematical objects which are both personal possessions and bits of the public world.[36] Foremost among such objects, and signs of all our later puzzlings over the elusive border between self and non-self, are the faeces, those prized, intimate products which the small child may withhold in a triumph of sadistic mastery, or lovingly surrender as gifts to the social world.[37] It is in the anal stage that we know for the first time the mixed delights of pleasurable retention and joyful self-squandering, the manipulation of our own bodily products for the sadistic control of others, the thrilling exploration of the fragile perimeter between what is 'proper' to us and to them. Through an erotic fissure in the replete body, products may emerge to dominate or cajole those around us, gifts which are also weapons, art-fully wrought communications than which nothing, after all, could be more natural. The pleasure of creating for its own sake, with no particular end in mind, mingles with the most calculatedly instrumental of emissions — just as the destructive thrill of self-undoing is overshadowed by the anxiety of loss.

Faeces, gift, exchange: it is possible to explore these

36 'On the Transformations of Instinct, as Exemplified in Anal Eroticism', *The Standard Edition of the Complete Psychological Works of Sigmund Freud* (London, 1953—73), vol. XVII.
37 My analogy between the letters of *Clarissa* and the faeces is not of course intended as a disguised value judgement on the novel. I have, however, august authority for this parallel:

> Leaving the bubbling beverage to cool,
> Fresca slips softly to the needful stool,
> Where the pathetic tale of Richardson
> Eases her labour till the deed is done.

(T. S. Eliot, *The Waste Land: a facsimile and transcript*, ed. Valerie Eliot (London, 1971), p. 23.)

Freudian interrelations a little further. For it is a form of faecal-like exchange — money — that lays the very infrastructure of modern societies, without whose anxious contestations over property — what is 'proper' to me or to another — the very plot of *Clarissa* would be unthinkable. It was Freud, not Marx, who wrote that 'the motive of human society is in the last resort an economic one';[38] it was Richardson, not a Marxist critic, who commented that the Harlowes' wrangling over property laid 'the foundation of the whole [novel] '.[39] Moreover, the patriarchal structure of all known societies is perhaps nowhere more evident than in the fact that the fundamental unit of exchange, the founding gift, is women.[40] In this sense, the letter of *Clarissa* can be seen not only as sign of female sexuality but as nothing less than *the woman herself*, that circulating property which cements the system of male dominance. What 'circulates' in the novel, what unifies its great circuits of textual exchange, is simply Clarissa herself, whether as daughter or lover, rival or confidante, protégée or property-owner. It is on the trading, withholding, surrendering or protecting of Clarissa that the currency of all that letter-writing is founded. The 'universal commodity' (Marx), magically unchanging in itself yet source of 'magical' transformations in others, 'pure gold' yet in ceaseless liquidity, Clarissa's body is itself the discourse of the text. It is the signifier which distributes others to their positions of power or desire, fixing them in some fraught relation to her own mysteriously inviolable being.

    To claim as much is to argue that Clarissa acts in the

38 'Introductory Lectures on Psychoanalysis', *Standard Edition*, vol. XVI, p. 312.

39 Postscript to *Clarissa*, vol. 4, p. 564.

40 See Irigaray, 'Des marchandises entre elles', *Ce sexe qui n'en est pas un*.

novel as the 'transcendental signifier'. Among the 'detachable' objects which Freud enumerates, one in particular exercises supreme force: the phallus itself, which the small child may fantasize as detachable from the body. 'The male organ,' write Laplanche and Pontalis, 'has a part to play in a series of interchangeable elements constituting "symbolic equations" (penis = faeces = child = gift, etc.); a common trait of these elements is that they are detachable from the subject and capable of circulating from one person to another.'[41] The phallus, too, is subject to circulation and exchange, as the lynch-pin of the patriarchal 'symbolic order'. In Freudian theory, the small boy will 'exchange' his incestuous desire for the mother for his future possession of this token of male power; the small girl will 'exchange' her desire to possess the phallus for the destiny of presenting a man with a child. If the phallus is thus what divides and differentiates, it nevertheless remains as an image mysteriously whole, unriven by the circuits of desire it sets in motion. And in so far as this, precisely, is Lovelace's fantastic image of Clarissa — that of a pure undivided ideal, at once source and prohibition of desire — it is possible to argue that Clarissa represents the phallus for this anxiety-ridden rake. The savage irony of *Clarissa* is that the sexual integrity of an independent woman can be imaged only in the fetishistic symbol of male power.

That Lovelace's sexual rapacity conceals a profound sexual anxiety need not, perhaps, be too clamorously argued. In a study of the Don Juan legend, Otto Rank has suggested that 'the characteristic Don Juan fantasy of conquering countless women, which has made the hero into a masculine ideal, is ultimately based on the unattainability of the mother and the compensatory substitute for

41 J. Laplanche and J.-B. Pontalis, *The Language of Psychoanalysis* (London, 1973), p. 313.

her....the many women whom he must always replace anew represent to him the *one* irreplaceable mother.'[42] Lovelace's self-appointed mission — to seduce, degrade and destroy as many women as possible — springs from a deep ambivalence towards what we may call, after Freud, the 'phallic woman'. Confronted in the Oedipal crisis by the truth that the mother 'lacks' a penis, the male child may assuage his own fears of castration by believing contradictorily that all people have a penis but some do not. By repressing the absence of the mother's 'castrated' penis, he may seek to restore it to her; but at the same time the woman's 'castration' serves to confirm his own masculinity, reflecting back his own 'fullness' in her 'lack'. Lovelace's pathological preoccupation with Clarissa shows something of this ambivalence. Daunted by her 'phallic' wholeness, shaken by this nameless threat to his own gender, Lovelace must possess Clarissa so that he may reunite himself with the lost phallus, and unmask her as reassuringly 'castrated'. Indeed by ritually exposing all women in turn, he may compulsively reassure himself that they are all indeed 'castrated'. All of them will be revealed as worthless, as easy prey to desire, in contrast with the one unattainable woman — the mother — who is beyond desire altogether. Yet since there are always more women to be degraded, the Oedipal anxiety is infinitely per-petuated, a self-generating script which brooks no closure. The one hope for closure is Clarissa: if even she, the 'representative' woman whose apparently unblemished self-identity is the very figure of the phallus, can be un-masked as no more than a whore, his Oedipal torment may be finally laid to rest. It is only by rupturing her body, dispersing her integrity into so many fragments, that Lovelace can steal back the phallus she represents to him and thus stabilize his own dangerously diffusive

42 *The Don Juan Legend* (Princeton, New Jersey, 1975), pp. 95, 41.

being. Clarissa, he complains at one point, has stolen his pen and is imitating his handwriting as a kind of superior *Doppelgänger* to himself. Yet this whole enterprise is ironically self-defeating, since by destroying Clarissa Lovelace risks destroying the phallus too. It is no wonder that he defers the rape unconscionably, dreading the loss of the very ideal he desires. There is no doubt that Lovelace deeply respects Clarissa, entranced by the very purity he loathes, furtively hoping that she may prove an intolerable exception to the rule that all women are dirt.

For Freud, the most usual device for denying the woman's 'castration' is the fetish. The fetish is always in some sense a substitute for the 'missing' female phallus – an object which, by plugging that alarming gap, will block the male's fantasy of his own possible mutilation. The fetish, as fantasmal phallus, is thus yet another of those 'detachable' objects, part of yet separable from the body like a scarf or shoe. Or, indeed, like a letter: there is surely no doubt that for Richardson and his characters writing is the greatest fetish of all. Portable and inanimate, yet imbued with all the living presence of a person, letters stand in for absent bodies, plug holes in physical inter-course, as surely as any piece of discarded underwear. What is the sign but a consoling stand-in for some removed piece of reality, at once concealing and supplementing that empty place? Pursued, protected, kissed, buried, wept over, physically assailed, letters in Richardson are the subject of a drama every bit as enthralling as any merely human adventure story. It is no glib aphorism to claim that the 'subject' of the text of *Clarissa* is, precisely, the text of *Clarissa*. And just as these letters are not 'really' substitutes – for what is Clarissa or Lovelace outside them? – so the sexual fetish 'stands in' for an object which was never more than fictional in the first place. This, indeed, is the irony of the epistolary novel – that if its gripping first-person immediacy dramatically intensifies the 'real', it also distances it, since all we have is a pile of letters endlessly referring to something else.[43]

The true fetish of *Clarissa*, however, is not exactly the letter but the person of Clarissa herself. As the 'phallic' woman, Clarissa is the totem by which Lovelace protects himself from his own terrible lack of being, even as she is the threat which creates that hollowness in the first place. In Lacanian terms, Clarissa figures for Lovelace as the Law or Name-of-the-Father, the censorious, castrating agency which places a taboo on the very desire it provokes into being. Lovelace is in this sense the victim of the ultimate male delusion, a hopeless prisoner of patriarchal false consciousness. His only hope is that, since Clarissa *is* the phallus, she cannot *have* it: his rape will not only denounce her as marked by the sign of castration but will itself actively accomplish that castration, fragment the phallus in dismembering her. This, as we have seen, is a purely self-defeating project; and it is thus not surprising that the rape of Clarissa initiates not only her own slow dying, but the utter disintegration of Lovelace himself. What finally thrusts him into despair and temporary psychosis is the unspeakable truth that Clarissa is not to be possessed. She is absolutely impenetrable, least of all by rape. Forced into this sole shocking encounter with the 'real', Lovelace's precarious self, fantasmal to the core, enters upon its steady dissolution.

In raping Clarissa he unmasks not the 'nothing' of her 'castration', but a rather more subversive absence: the

---

43 John Preston, in *The Created Self: The Reader's Role in Eighteenth Century Fiction* (London, 1970), sees well enough that 'The book is made up of documents, and the documents are what the book is about' (p. 53). He also sees this as a form of tragic alienation, since 'What the process of reading in itself cannot offer is a living relationship' (p. 81). This is a perceptive, but also perhaps too 'humanist' reading: it overlooks that strand in Richardson which sees writing as a more ideal mutuality than physical intercourse.

reality of the woman's body, a body which resists all representation and remains stubbornly recalcitrant to his fictions.[44] The 'real' of *Clarissa* — the point around which this elaborate two thousand page text pivots — is the rape; yet the rape goes wholly unrepresented, as the hole at the centre of the novel towards which this huge mass of writing is sucked only to sheer off again. Indeed one ingenious commentator has doubted whether the rape ever happened at all.[45] Lovelace's sexual climax is also the novel's great anticlimax, a purely impersonal act of violence which refuses entry into discourse and brusquely unveils language for what it is: a ceaselessly digressive supplement which, *pace* Richardson's own ideology of the sign, will never succeed in nailing down the real. On the other hand, the non-representation of the rape highlights the centrality of discourse: in a view of sexuality more typical of women than of men, it suggests that without sympathy and affection the physical act itself is relatively trivial. The violated body of Clarissa slips through the net of writing to baffle representation; as Lovelace's frantic assault on the very scandal of *meaning*, the rape defies signification for reasons other than those of literary decorum. Lovelace's post-structuralist fictions stand revealed in their true gratuitousness: they are powerless to inscribe the 'real' of the woman's body, that outer limit upon all language. There has been no out-manoeuvring Clarissa in speech, of which she is mistress, but a direct onslaught on her body proves just as profitless. Lovelace will never discover 'where the dear creature puts her letters', never lay bare the springs of her subjectivity. Clarissa, after the rape, refers to her own body more than once as 'nothing', a declaration which critics have read as

44 See Montrelay, *L'ombre et le nom*.
45 See Judith Wilt, 'He Could Go No Farther: A Modest Proposal about Lovelace and Clarissa', *PMLA* 92 (1), 1977.

no more than a puritan repudiation of the flesh;[46] but the implications of this denial cut deeper. It must be taken together with her assertion that 'I am nobody's': a radical refusal of any place within the 'symbolic order', a rebuffing of all patriarchal claims over her person. The dying Clarissa is nothing, errant, schizoid, a mere empty place and non-person; her body occasions writing — her will, the whole text of the novel — but is itself absent from it, and will be literally nothing when we come to read the book. *Clarissa*, like another, rather more influential text of Western history, is the testimony left to a dead, consecrated body. The subject Clarissa is that which escapes, obstinately self-identical, as in some frustrating fantasy where an ever-fragmenting medium always inexorably reunites. And what has actually escaped is nothing less than the unconscious which Clarissa's body signifies for Lovelace — that un-appropriable Other whose place is to be always elsewhere.

If more evidence were needed of Lovelace's Oedipal difficulties, there is always the astonishing dream which he recounts to Belford after the rape — a dream in which the figure of a 'good' mother changes rapidly into a perse-cuting, vindictive one, and that in turn into Lovelace himself.[47] This baffling, bottomlessly interpretable dream-text, worth a whole study in itself, exhibits one striking general feature: what, after Freud, we may call the 'poly-morphous perversity' of Lovelace himself. Mother, father, child, lover; transsexuality; sibling and parental incest: in a dizzying exchange of positions, a constant process of

46 See, for example, Allan Wendt, 'Clarissa's Coffin', *Philological Quarterly* 39, 1960.
47 See vol. 3, pp. 248—51. Any adequate interpretation of this dream would need to relate Freud's exploration of the Oedipal crisis to Melanie Klein's analysis of the infant's pre-Oedipal ambiva-lence towards the mother, a theme deeply marked in the text. (See Klein, *Love, Guilt and Reparation and Other Works* (London, 1975).)

splitting, projection, condensation and displacement, Lovelace comes in his dream to assume all these roles and practices in turn, with the same protean movement which marks his pen. The dream reveals Clarissa as unconscious mother-figure for Lovelace, which in turn makes it possible to see how the incest prohibition may be partly responsible for his long-deferred seduction of her. She bears him a son, who is at once Lovelace's own son and Lovelace himself, so that in a common Oedipal fantasy he triumphantly becomes his own father. By the end of the dream, he has successfully resolved his relationship with the ambivalently threatening and nurturing mother, reaffirmed his own masculine power by impregnating Clarissa, and punctured her own infuriating narcissism in the process. It is no wonder that Lovelace, having reified Clarissa to the phallus, stands in such awe of her: for the phallus is the centrepiece of the 'symbolic order', that stable system of gender roles which he is for the most part unable to enter. His 'feminine' writing is one sign of a bisexuality which relates him to a tradition of Satan as hermaphrodite.[48] Thoroughly narcissistic and regressive, Lovelace's 'rakishness', for all its virile panache, is nothing less than a crippling incapacity for adult sexual relationship. His misogyny and infantile sadism achieve their appropriate expression in the virulently anti-sexual act of rape. It is this pathetic character who has been celebrated by the critics as Byronic hero, Satanic vitalist or post-modernist artist.

Clarissa is the story of a young woman of outstanding kindness, virtue and intelligence who is made to suffer

48 See Hagstrum, *Sex and Sensibility*, p. 45.

under a violently oppressive family, is tricked away from home by a notorious sexual predator, deceived, imprisoned, persecuted, drugged and raped, and finally impelled to her death. What have the critics made of this narrative?

Dorothy van Ghent's classic essay on the novel begins by noting that its central action, the rape, 'might have assumed a position of minor importance among Moll [Flanders's] adventures in adultery, bigamy and incest — conceivably an incident that Moll might even have forgotten to make a "memorandum" of'.[49] Considered in the abstract, van Ghent comments, 'the deflowering of a young lady' represents 'a singularly thin and unrewarding piece of action ... and one which scarcely seems to deserve the universal uproar which it provokes in the book'.[50] Van Ghent has great fun with Clarissa's torture at the hands of Lovelace — 'Clarissa on her knees in prayer in miraculously dirt-resistant white garments, or Clarissa in torn clothes and with streaming eyes, prostrated at the feet of her demon-lover' — and manages to imply that she deserves what she gets: 'The womanly quality which Richardson has made attractive in these images is that of an erotically tinged debility which offers, masochistically, a ripe temptation to violence.'[51] Pausing to compare the image of Clarissa with a *Vogue* cover-girl ('a wraith of clothes, debile and expensive, irrelevant to sense-life or affectional life'),[52] or 'the many-breasted woman with torn dishabille and rolling eyeballs' on the cover of detective stories ('she is to be vicariously ripped and murdered'), van Ghent goes on to scoff at 'virginal, high-minded, helpless womanhood' and remarks, falsely, that chastity in

49 *The English Novel: Form and Function* (New York, 1961), p. 45.
50 ibid., p. 47.
51 ibid., p. 49.
52 ibid., p. 51.

Clarissa is a physical attribute.[53] *Clarissa* is not a tragedy, she considers, because it ends happily in the heroine's attainment of heaven. Clarissa 'goes off' with Lovelace as an act of daughterly rebellion (she is in fact *tricked* into elopement, a fact which Ian Watt also obscures), and the novel finally endorses the values of 'parental authoritarianism in the family, and the cash nexus as the only binding tie for society at large'.[54] Clarissa herself is an image of 'perverted sexuality' and 'the sterilization of instinct': her death is a ma`abre ritual, a 'common orgy' in which 'she performs her [death throes] charmingly'. Van Ghent quotes approvingly V. S. Pritchett's comment in *The Living Novel* that Clarissa 'represents that extreme of puritanism which desires to be raped. Like Lovelace's her sexuality is really violent, insatiable in its wish for destruction.'[55] The whole novel is no more than a rapist's wish-fulfilment, the fascinating motif of 'the carnal assault on a virgin'; its imagery renders 'defloration exciting and attractive'. The essay's final gesture, unsurprisingly, is to put in a word for the squirearchy: Lovelace is the work's 'whipping boy' for its own hypocritically disowned indulgences.

Most literary critics, Raymond Williams once remarked, are natural cavaliers;[56] but even van Ghent's hard-boiled scepticism appears pious when placed beside William Beatty Warner's *Reading Clarissa*, a fashionably deconstructionist piece out to vilify Clarissa and sing the virtues of her rapist. Clarissa, as we have seen, holds to a severely

---

53 This is a common error of critics: Leslie Fiedler believes that 'Clarissa is, indeed, indistinguishable from her virginity' (*Love and Death in the American Novel*, p. 64), and David Daiches, who thinks Clarissa is 'silly', holds that 'Richardson had a purely technical view of chastity' (*Literary Essays* (London, 1956), p. 47).
54 *The English Novel*, p. 61.
55 ibid.
56 *The Long Revolution* (London, 1961), p. 256.

representational ideology of writing, trusts in the stable sign and the unitary self, and subscribes to the values of truth, coherence and causality; Lovelace, by contrast, is a proto-Nietzschean who celebrates plurality, groundlessness and *jouissance*. It seems logical, then, that a contemporary deconstructionist should find Lovelace the hero and Clarissa the villain, without allowing a little matter like rape to modify his judgement. 'By winning our laughter and giving us pleasure, Lovelace helps to undo the matrix of truth and value through which Clarissa would have us see, know and judge.'[57] The rapist is merely a Derridean jester misunderstood: 'There is an artistry and economy in Lovelace's use of the lie. But beyond this, the lie has a peculiar aptness for use in an assault on Clarissa. If Lovelace can get Clarissa to live within an acknowledged lie at Sinclair's — like the notion that she is his wife — he can disrupt the ground of her self-complacence.'[58] It is difficult to see what 'lie' signifies for Warner in the first place, since he does not of course subscribe to the boring old metaphysical bugbear of 'truth'; but it certainly serves to excuse Lovelace's action of imprisoning Clarissa in a brothel once we realize that this is a salutary deconstruction of her metaphysical delusions, a radical, perhaps even comradely, gesture. Warner, who finds Clarissa's sisterly friendship with Anna Howe 'chill and uninteresting',[59] regards Lovelace as 'defer[ring] any drastic step, like rape or marriage, that might simplify their relationship',[60] though he does not develop this intriguingly original ground for objecting to rape. He concedes that Clarissa in the brothel is 'imprisoned, surrounded by evil, and in danger of violation',[61]

57 *Reading Clarissa*, p. 30.
58 ibid., p. 32.
59 ibid., p. 39.
60 ibid.
61 ibid., p. 42.

but judiciously mutes these realities to an 'image of virtue in distress', which sounds less unpleasant. The best way to deconstruct Clarissa's tediously unified self is, in fact, to rape her: 'rape is the most cogent response to Clarissa's fictional projection of herself as a whole unified body "full of light"'. [Lovelace] can subvert this fiction by introducing a small part of himself *into* Clarissa. Thus the rape, like all Lovelace's displacements, will seek to induce the slight difference that will make all the difference.'[62] Lovelace, whom Warner finds 'charming', moves towards the rape 'with an inexorable necessity': what else can the poor fellow do if he is out to deconstruct her? His deceptive enticing of Clarissa from her home is just 'Lovelace's joke'; the violence of his rape is less 'insidious' than the 'will to power' which compels Clarissa herself to write her story, enamoured as she is of old-style ontological claptrap like truth, meaning, narrative and causality. Lovelace's 'shortcomings', Warner writes, 'are not held against him by the lover of comedy';[63] Clarissa, presumably, couldn't take a joke, although Warner does generously acknowledge that 'something genuinely arresting' happened to her when she was drugged and raped, and informs us that, having been raped, she 'feels used'. It is not, however, that she has been used by a sexual oppressor, but by 'Lovelace's fictional machinery'. Warner greatly relishes Lovelace's unspeakably cynical defence of the rape of his 'pretty little miss', and regards most critics as conspiring with the prim Clarissa to judge Lovelace in such shabbily undeconstructed terms as 'seriousness, consistency, sympathy, maturity, a full deep heart, and belief in the "real"'.[64] His book is an ominous exposé of the truly reactionary nature of much deconstructionist 'radicalism', once divorced from the social and

62 ibid., p. 49.
63 ibid., p. 80.
64 ibid., p. 268.

political contexts it so characteristically finds hard to handle.

Not all critics, gratifyingly, have been as flagrantly prejudiced or obtusely unhistorical as Warner and van Ghent. But even as judicious and illuminating a study of the novel as Ian Watt's is not without its symptomatic blind spots. Watt, at least, sees that Clarissa's virginity is in no sense a commodity, for if it were then Lovelace would have been right to believe that 'once overcome [is] for ever overcome', and as he discovers to his cost, this is not so. He is also right to point out, as most critics do, that Clarissa is dangerously unclear and to some degree self-deceiving about her initial feelings for Lovelace: 'we are fully entitled to suspect Clarissa herself of not knowing her own feelings; and Lovelace is not altogether wrong in suspecting her of the "female affectation of denying [her] love".'[65] Not *altogether* wrong; but within a few pages this emotional *ambiguity* in Clarissa has unquestioningly become her 'unconscious love' for Lovelace,[66] and on the following page, with gathering dogmatic certainty, Clarissa's utterly well-grounded doubts about her seducer have become spuriously equated with his own 'false sexual ideology'. Once this move has been made, the ground is cleared for a reckless comparison of what are now the 'star-crossed lovers' Clarissa and Lovelace to the great romantic tragedies of Romeo and Juliet or Tristan and Isolde. The implication is clear, and common: Clarissa and Lovelace are equally cocooned in false consciousness, mutually thwarting and travestying; how tragic that they were unable to liberate one another's real selves. This, to be sure, contains a seed of truth; but it obscures the fact that

65 *The Rise of the Novel*, p. 238.
66 Cynthia Griffin Wolff, in her highly interesting study, speaks of Clarissa's 'adoration' of Lovelace, a strange hyperbole (*Samuel Richardson and the Eighteenth Century Puritan Character*, p. 96).

Lovelace, far from figuring as some Romeo in wolf's clothing, is for the most part simply a wolf, and is perceived by Clarissa to be so. To suggest a symmetry between Clarissa's partial, understandable self-deceptions and Lovelace's unremitting schizoid fantasies is to cast a slur upon Clarissa.

In support of his attempt to convict Clarissa of collusion in the rape, Watt predictably quotes her delirious ramblings after the event:

> A lady took a great fancy to a young lion, or a bear, I forget which — but of a bear, or a tiger, I believe it was. It was made her a present of when a whelp. She fed it with her own hand: she nursed up the wicked cub with great tenderness; and would play with it without fear or apprehension of danger ... But mind what followed: at last, somehow, neglecting to satisfy its hungry maw, or having otherwise disobliged it on some occasion, it resumed its nature; and on a sudden fell upon her, and tore her in pieces. And who was most to blame, I pray? The brute, or the lady? The lady, surely! for what *she* did was *out* of nature, *out* of character, at least: what it did was *in* its own nature.[67]

This, written directly after the rape has occurred, must of course be read in the light of the irrational guilt women commonly experience after such violations. Even then, however, it will hardly bear close scrutiny. Lovelace was not made a present of Clarissa's 'when a whelp', if this means that she originally thought him innocuous; on the contrary, her suspicions of him date back to their earliest encounters. She never 'nursed him up with great tenderness', or 'play[ed] with [him] without fear or apprehension

67   vol. 3, p. 206.

of danger': she treated him with proper vigilance from the outset. The lady was not in fact to blame; Clarissa's self-castigation is quite unjustified. The passage commonly quoted to demonstrate a rare moment of self-insight on her part in fact reveals a self-lacerating mystification. The rape has simply thrust her more deeply into ideological submission. If Watt's judgement, generally so exact, is inaccurate here, it is equally so in his assertion that 'Clarissa dies rather than recognize the flesh.'[68] On the contrary, she dies because she has recognized it all too well.

The view of Clarissa as neurotic prude has become the merest commonplace of Richardson criticism. Irwin Gopnik can write *en passant*, unarguedly, of her 'naïve, adolescent, morbidly self-pitying, sublime idealism',[69] and Leslie Fiedler writes airily of the book's 'pornographic' aspects. Eaves and Kimpel rightly retort that anybody reading *Clarissa* for this reason is in for a disappointment: 'We see very little sex in it, surprisingly little considering the story.'[70] 'One cannot but sympathize with [Clarissa's] demand [to be treated as a person],' they write, adding with remarkable liberality of spirit that 'even today, a young girl who does not want to be raped ought not to be raped.'[71] (The implications of that 'even today' are interesting: even in these permissive times when young girls may well not care whether they are raped or not, it is obligatory to abstain.) Eaves and Kimpel's moral generosity does not, however, stretch to sympathy with the important, largely suppressed current of women's writing which was influenced by Richardson: 'We are not much concerned,' they announce, 'with his influence on a few second-rate sentimental females.'[72]

68 *The Rise of the Novel*, p. 247.
69 *A Theory of Style and Richardson's 'Clarissa'*, p. 90.
70 *Samuel Richardson*, p. 258.
71 ibid., p. 105.
72 ibid., p. 611.

It is now possible to see why *Clarissa* has proved such a scandalous text for modern criticism. It deeply offends the fashionable liberal assumption that virtue is boring, the banality that the devil has all the best tunes. For here is a novel whose protagonist is not only kind, chaste and conscientious but also embarrassingly rich and real. Lovelace is also, of course, a magnificently realized character; but the devil-worshipping critics have to struggle hard to suppress the fact that, as Eaves and Kimpel argue, 'Whatever of himself Richardson put into Lovelace, he rejected, and not merely in a conventional moralistic way, but with a side of his mind as deep and at least as important as the side which was able to realize Lovelace.'[73] Effectively ignored throughout the nineteenth century, Richardson stages a comeback when a more sophisticated criticism comes to discern that Clarissa is not all she is cracked up to be. Suavely 'knowing' analyses become possible once Clarissa's faults are triumphantly unmasked — once it is seen that she is after all spiritually proud, dangerously unclear about her own deeper feelings, prey to a certain moral *hauteur* and self-admiration, irritatingly inflexible at unpropitious moments and prone to masochistic self-abasement. Once the spicy news is out that the madonna has feet of clay — that she is, after all, a woman, with sexual impulses and moral failings — an avenging male iconoclasm moves in. The way is then clear for the cavaliers, deconstructionists and debunking liberals to insinuate that Clarissa is only a little less reprehensible than Roxana. In this, as usual, Richardson had pre-empted his critics: he writes that he had deliberately given his heroine moral defects to make her more convincing.[74] Clarissa is indeed far from a madonna: her treatment of Lovelace can be exasperatingly perverse, her moral

73 ibid., p. 260.
74 *Selected Letters*, p. 101.

self-assurance repellent, her denial of her own sexual instincts seriously damaging. But even when the most damning evidence has been gleefully summoned for the prosecution, it remains, on balance, remarkably feeble. 'The minor reticences and confusions revealed in the feminine correspondence,' writes Ian Watt, 'are insignificant compared to the much grosser discrepancies between Lovelace's pretended attitude to Clarissa and the falsehoods and trickeries which his letters reveal.'[75] The ideological benefits to be reaped from discrediting Clarissa are considerable. For it allows criticism to fend off the sheer radicalism of this astonishing text, and whole generations of students to believe, amazingly, that 'one of the greatest of the unread novels' (Christopher Hill) is not only unendurably long but priggish, preachy and pornographic to boot.

Some of the charges against Clarissa — that she is prudish, dull, naïve, chronically idealizing or tediously meek — seem to me merely false. Other accusations — that she is responsible for her own rape, or that she is fit meat for voyeurs — are not only false but, so to speak, slanderous. Still other criticisms — that she is morbid, masochistic and narcissistic — are true in a sense, but rarely in the sense in which they are intended. Such upbraidings are in any case typically exaggerated: they apply more to the protracted scenes of Clarissa's dying than to her earlier career. And it is of course just these amazing scenes — in which Clarissa holds public audience on her death bed, orders her coffin and writes letters upon it, attends with quiet efficiency to the last detail of her testament and interment — which have provoked the mocking incredulity of the critical cavaliers. That tell-tale device on Clarissa's coffin — a serpent with its tail in its mouth — has been busily enough annotated, as 'emblem of an endlessly self-consuming

75 *The Rise of the Novel*, p. 239.

sexual desire' (Watt), sign of a sterile narcissism. But narcissism, as Lear remarked about low voices, is an excellent thing in a woman. What struck the patriarchal Freud as particularly regressive in women — their 'cat-like' proneness to sensual self-delight, their cool, self-fulfilling independence of male desire — are precisely the qualities which patriarchy is unable to countenance.[76] Female narcissism is not only scandalous but fearful: it allows men a glimpse of that terrifying condition in which woman might be independent of them. It is by virtue of her profound narcissism, not by dint of being fetishized to the phallus, that Clarissa is finally able to slip through the net of male desire and leave the hands of Lovelace and her family empty. Her elaborate dying is a ritual of deliberate disengagement from patriarchal and class society, a calculated 'decathecting' of that world whereby libidinal energy is gradually withdrawn from its fruitless social investments into her own self. Dorothy van Ghent, predictably, finds this farcically distasteful: 'The scene in the death room is an astonishing one. The room is crowded with people, all pressing around the dying woman to obtain her blessing. The mourning is as public as possible; every sigh, every groan, every tear is recorded. One is given to understand that nothing could be a greater social good than Clarissa's death, nothing could be more enjoyable than to watch her in her death throes (she performs them charmingly), nothing a greater privilege than to be present at this festival of death and to weep and sniffle in the common

---

76 See Freud, 'On Narcissism: An Introduction', *Standard Edition*, vol. XIV. But see also, for a feminist valorizing of female narcissism, Ulrike Prokop, *Weiblichen Lebenszusammenhäng* (Frankfurt am Main, 1976), Sarah Kofman, *L'Énigme de la femme* (Paris, 1981), and Janine Chasseguet-Smirgel, 'Feminine Guilt and the Oedipus Complex', in *Female Sexuality*, ed. Chasseguet-Smirgel (Ann Arbor, 1970).

orgy.'[77] Twentieth-century academics do not of course commonly die in public, and so may be forgiven for finding this spectacle indecorous. Van Ghent would presumably have Clarissa a Little Nell, expiring in decent privacy. But the public nature of Clarissa's death is the whole point: her dying is in a profound sense a political gesture, a shocking, surreal act of resignation from a society whose power system she has seen in part for what it is.[78] It would be considerably too convenient for the ruling class to make of her death a hole-in-the-corner affair. The death is a properly collective event, a complex, material business, a negation of society which is also, curiously, a living part of it. Clarissa is no Lady of Shallot but a saint and martyr — that is to say, one whose life has been lifted out of the merely private arena into the public sphere, in an exemplary liturgical action whose end is to involve and transform others. Richardson is not to be contrasted as a novelist of the 'personal' with his 'social' rival Henry Fielding.[79] Every sigh, groan and tear must indeed be duly recorded, taken down in writing and used as damning documentary evidence against a society where the rape of a Clarissa is possible. That scrupulous record is, of course, the novel *Clarissa* itself. Clarissa's death is indeed intended as a 'great social good', tragic though it remains, and there is certainly both pleasure and privilege in being allowed to participate in it. But the pleasure is less that

77 *The English Novel*, p. 60.

78 'Clarissa is a champion of the downtrodden woman of her day and all days' (Jean H. Hagstrum, *Sex and Sensibility*, p. 206). This — a note rarely struck in Richardson criticism — comes within what is in general one of the finest recent accounts of the novel.

79 A commonplace of Richardson criticism: see Leo Braudy's extraordinary claim that 'In *Clarissa* society has effectively vanished and the battleground is inside the self' ('Penetration and Impenetrability in *Clarissa*', in *New Aspects of the Eighteenth Century*, ed. Philip Harth (New York and London, 1974), p. 186).

of a morbid voyeurism than of an appropriate sadism: every symptom of Clarissa's saintliness, every sign that she is intelligently in command of her dying and utterly autonomous of others, is a nail, not in her own coffin, but in that of the society which has driven her to her death and must now stand by, guilty, horror-stricken and ineffectually repentant. Who indeed would not find these scenes deeply enjoyable, with an eye to their devastating effects on Lovelace and the Harlowes? Clarissa, to adopt van Ghent's sarcastic term, does indeed 'perform' her death; that, precisely, is the point.

That which is purely itself, like the self-gratifying narcissist, cannot be represented. For representation involves spacing, division, an articulation of signs, and it is this which Clarissa finally denies. Brooding upon her own being, rapt in an 'imaginary' relationship to her own death, she refuses incorporation into social discourse and transforms herself instead into a pure self-referential sign. Her death is thus the consummation of her ideology of writing: in dying, she achieves that pure transparency of signifier to signified which she seeks in the integrity of her script. Such transparency — the baffling enigma of that which is merely itself — is bound to appear socially opaque, a worthless tautology or resounding silence. There is nothing to be done with it, as the patriarchs can finally do nothing with Clarissa, the stubborn little minx who perversely insists upon dying and leaving them with blood on their hands. When all the voices are crying for compromise, Clarissa moves steadfastly into her death, as courteously unheeding of this clamouring as her author was of those readers who begged for a marriage to Lovelace and a happy ending. In refusing this compromise, Richardson cunningly pressed the Christian ideology of his audience to its intolerable limits: if you really believe a heavenly reward is the ultimate good, why would you have Clarissa live? The more transparent Clarissa becomes, the less legible she is, for such an unbroken identity of purpose must in the end have the inscrutability of a cypher. Her 'morbid' death wish remains unswerving, for in this society death is indeed the only place of inviolable security. Her 'masochism' is complete, for she has understood well enough that this is no society for a woman to live in. It is no accident that the liberal critics, who find such masochism and morbidity a little unhealthy, should be equally blind to the radicalism of that political insight.

What Clarissa's death signifies, in fact, is an absolute refusal of political society: sexual oppression, bourgeois patriarchy and libertine aristocracy together.[80] If Lovelace is unable fully to enter the symbolic order in the first place, Clarissa is the 'transcendental signifier' who ends up by opting out of it. She is not, needless to say, some feminist or historical materialist *avant la lettre*: nobody could be more submissive to patriarchal order, more eloquent an ideologue of bourgeois pieties, than Clarissa Harlowe. It is hard for the modern reader to hear the litany of posthumous praises sung to her unbelievably upright existence without feeling a wild surge of iconoclasm. Yet each item of that litany, each tedious piece of testimony to Clarissa's impeccable moralism and conformism, simply twists the dagger a little deeper in the very social order of which she was so fine a flower. The more the novel underwrites those values, the more it exposes the Harlowes; the more meekly bourgeois Clarissa is revealed to be, the more devastating grows the critique of those who did her to death. There seems little doubt that in the prolonged detail of the death scenes the text

80 I use the term 'bourgeois' here in a broad sense: strictly speaking, the Harlowes are gentry, as indeed is Lovelace. But Lovelace has close aristocratic connections and lives an aristocratic ideology, whereas the Harlowes, although in no sense social upstarts, are closer ideologically to the middle class.

unleashes upon Clarissa a sadistic violence which belongs with its Lovelacian unconscious. But the more it punishes her, the more virtuous she is made to appear, and so the more savage becomes the indictment of Lovelace and the Harlowes. The death scenes become the medium whereby Lovelace's sadism may be turned against himself, and harnessed to bring low the bourgeoisie into the bargain. Bourgeois ideology is made to stand shamefaced and threadbare in the light of its own doctrines. The impossibly ideal nature of Clarissa's virtue is indeed beyond realism, a kind of grave parody of official moral ideology which, by pressing it to an intolerable extreme, begins to betray something of its corrupt reality.

It is not only that Clarissa exposes the rift between bourgeois pieties and bourgeois practice; it is also that those pieties themselves, once submitted to the pressures of fictional form, begin to crack open. 'It is Richardson's greatness,' writes Christopher Hill, '... that his respect for Clarissa's integrity led him to push the Puritan code forward to the point at which its flaw was completely revealed, at which it broke down as a standard for conduct for this world. His *conscious* desire in writing the novel was to assert the bourgeois and Puritan conception of marriage against the feudal—cavalier standards of Lovelace and the Harlowe emphasis on concentration of property. But the contradictions of subordination in equality which were inherent in the Puritan view of women were too strong for him.'[81] Richardson, who in private life argued against full sexual equality and thought polygamy a possible option, is constrained by the logic of his own fiction to throw that whole ideology into radical question. Like Clarissa, his pen exceeds his intentions, conjuring a levelling sub-text from beneath the carefully policed script of his

81 'Clarissa Harlowe and her Times', *Essays in Criticism* 5, 1955, pp. 334—5.

novel. Standard Christian values are pitted against 'parental authoritarianism and the cash-nexus', which van Ghent absurdly takes to be the novel's positive values; but then, in a further antithesis concealed within this opposition, those values of female subordination are themselves interrogated by an altogether more subversive voice. It is a voice most evident in the comradely correspondence between Clarissa and Anna Howe. Anna is no feminist paradigm — she believes, for example, that 'our sex are best dealt with by boisterous and unruly spirits' — but she is perhaps one of the nearest things to a militant separatist that the eighteenth-century novel has to offer:

> Upon my word, I most heartily despise that sex! I wish they would let our fathers and mothers alone; teasing *them* to tease *us* with their golden promises, and protestations, and settlements, and the rest of their ostentatious nonsense. How charmingly might you and I live together, and despise them all! But to be cajoled, wire-drawn, and ensnared, like silly birds into a state of bondage or vile subordination: to be courted as princesses for a few weeks, in order to be treated as slaves for the rest of our lives. Indeed, my dear, as you say of Solmes, I cannot endure them![82]

Caustic, humorous and debunking, unswerving in sisterly solidarity yet astringently critical, Anna is part of Clarissa's own unconscious, able to articulate that which it would be improper for the heroine herself to voice.

Clarissa is mildly scandalized by Anna's high-handed treatment of her suitor Mr Hickman, and gently reproves her for this injuriousness. Hickman is a good man, and in this sense Anna's behaviour is certainly unwarranted; but there is more at stake in the sexual power struggle than

82 vol. 1, p. 131.

one man's sensibilities, and to this extent Anna's lack of charity is politically justified. Clarissa, typically, adheres to absolute standards of truth and justice; Anna shrewdly recognizes that such values are indissociable from the shifting power strategies in which they are embedded. To be false or unjust, in conditions where the other has the power advantage, may be a productive error, as near to 'genuine' truth and justice as one can get. Clarissa's 'representational' model of truth, as fixed correspondence between discourse and reality, overlooks the fact that truth is always a matter of power and position, a function of social relations, an effect of particular discourses in particular conditions. How are women to live by truth and justice in a society where the very criteria for defining what counts as such are already in the hands of patriarchy? What is the value of truth when like the confessional letter it merely delivers you over to oppression and so perpetuates a pervasive falsity? *Clarissa* implicitly poses to political society a question which shakes it to the roots: can truth and power be compatible? Can one trust simply to the 'literal' truth of one's discourse and discount its mystifying effects? Or can one falsehood be countered only by another more fruitful falsehood, which in shifting the balance of power in one's favour may bring a deeper demystification to birth? Can those who are stripped of power from the outset, excluded by the rules of discourse from full subjecthood, enter the power game at all without being instantly falsified? And is it any less misinterpretable to stay silent?

The great warring of discourses that is *Clarissa*, in which statements are minefields and paragraphs political tactics, turns upon such fundamental questions. It is as a struggle over meanings, a wary negotiating of nuances and implications, that the battle between the classes and the sexes is conducted. There is hardly a proposition in the book that is not refracted through the play of power interests, saturated to its roots by strategic considerations, bristling with tactical manoeuvres. To write is to gain a toe-hold in the power struggle, a continual skirmishing and out-flanking. In this, Richardson resembles no writer quite so much as his admirer Henry James. For those who enter upon this dangerous game with a handicap — their sex — nothing is more important than the code of propriety, which is at once something less than the whole truth and an indispensable set of defences without which no truth could survive. In modern parlance, the code serves as a kind of 'problematic', the shared invisible underside of all utterances, the matrix which determines their status as acceptable discourse. Alan McKillop writes of Clarissa's 'excessive propriety',[83] but the short answer to that is Ian Watt's: 'As a result of these revelations [Lovelace's trickeries], we realize that the code which might seem to make Clarissa too prudent is not prudent enough when measured against the outrageous means which men allow themselves to gain their ends.'[84] When Mark Kinkead-Weekes complains with some justice that Clarissa is at certain times too undiplomatic, too stiffly unyielding in her dealings with Lovelace, we feel entitled to ask what could possibly count as excessive vigilance in addressing a man who has just raped you? Indeed, one of the novel's strengths is that it seems ready to risk the charge of 'overniceness' in Clarissa, even to the point of her becoming unsympathetic — that it accepts this as an unavoidable 'bind', an untenable but essential position into which vice manipulates virtue.

Clarissa's own faith is that truth and propriety are not fundamentally at odds. As in the Janus-faced letter, at once nature and artifice, it is the code itself which should

83 *The Early Masters of English Fiction* (Kansas and London, 1962), p. 73.
84 *The Rise of the Novel*, p. 239.

determine how 'free' you can be. Clarissa's letters are for the most part political gestures in just this sense, scrupulous alignments of tactics and truthfulness. If Belford admires her as a 'lady scrupulously strict to *her* word, incapable of art or design',[85] this indifferent novelist is also after all the woman capable of penning on her death-bed the most Lovelacian *double entendre* of all, in her true but grossly misleading comment that she is about to depart for her 'Father's house'. This blending of sincerity and deception is a necessity for the oppressed: Anna Howe remarks on the dangers of a woman writing her heart to a man practised in deceit. Truth may not be compatible with virtue: it is virtuous to forgive another's faults, but Clarissa's excuses for her vicious bully of a brother ('...really a worthy young man, but perhaps a little too headstrong in his first resentments and conceptions of things'[86]) amount to wholesale distortion. It is equally virtuous to be humble, but humility for Clarissa often enough means false self-accusation. It is by trusting to the possibility of disinterested truth that she falls foul of Lovelace in the first place. Lovelace has been maligned by the Harlowes, so Clarissa feels compelled to speak up for him in the name of an objective justice: 'It is then the call of justice, as I may say, to speak a little in favour of a man, who, although provoked by my brother, did not do him all the mischief he could have done him, and which my brother had endeavoured to do *him*.'[87] This is in any case rationalizing, as Clarissa already finds Lovelace sexually attractive: her impartial intervention is considerably more interested than she admits. Once victimized by her family and abducted by Lovelace, she will soon discover that enunciations of truth and justice are not to be

85　vol. 2, p. 159.
86　vol. 4, p. 354.
87　vol. 1, p. 136.

so easily disengaged from the power interests and social relations which frame them. As with Richardson's own struggles with literary form, she will see the problem of reconciling such judicious metalanguage with the passions and prejudices of the moment.

What Clarissa will discover in particular is the most demoralizing double bind of all: the truth that it is not so easy to distinguish resistance to power from collusion with it. There is no way she can escape from Lovelace without talking to him, and to talk is to create a certain complicity. If Clarissa negotiates she is guilty of compromise; if she refuses to bargain her position becomes even more untenable. Power reproduces itself by engendering in its victims a collusion which is the very condition of their survival. Few people are likely to bulk larger in a woman's life than the man who has raped her: even the ruthlessly impersonal act of rape cannot help generating between Clarissa and Lovelace something that might genuinely be called a bond. This is not to lend credence to the offensive suggestion that Clarissa desires her own violation; it is simply to question the sentimental, characteristically male notion that women are the mere passive victims of men's power. As Michèle Barrett has written: 'An analysis of gender ideology in which women are always innocent, always passive victims of patriarchal power, is patently not satisfactory.'[88] Lovelace's exercise of power is bound to evoke countervailing tactics in Clarissa, if she is to survive at all; she is thus drawn onto the terrain of a conflict in which she will always be the loser because the rules disadvantage her from the outset. To protect her own position means submitting to a struggle which jeopardizes it at every step. What critics have read, often rightly, as her pride, self-will, artfulness or inflexibility are inseparable from this fact. The novel sees well enough that if virtue is

88 *Women's Oppression Today* (London, 1980), p. 110.

necessary it is also an encumbrance, since to behave well in a predatory society is the surest way to unleash its violence.

What will finally strike Lovelace impotent, however, is the fact that he cannot secure Clarissa's collusion. His own tactics are parasitic on Clarissa's counter-moves: it is the thrill of the chase he finds most erotic, a sadistic delight in the prey whose very pain forces her to respond. Clarissa's pleadings thus fuel the very force they are intended to check. But once Lovelace is reduced to the humiliating gesture of having to drug his victim in order to rape her, he has lost the war even before he has performed the act. A forced victory is no victory at all: Lovelace can hardly demonstrate that all women are secretly lecherous if Clarissa is unconscious at the crucial moment. In a sense nobody experiences the rape: not the reader, not the comatose Clarissa, not even Lovelace, for whom the act is purely empty. As in Hegel's great myth of master and slave, Locelace requires from Clarissa the very autonomy he finds unbearable; to quell her freedom is to undermine himself. To recognize that master and victim are always somehow complicit may induce a certain political pessimism, but it may also do the opposite: the fact that the dependence is not all one way is, in this novel at least, what will bring the ruling class low.

Clarissa's 'representational' model of truth, which abstracts truth from its strategic contexts, is exposed by the novel as severely limited. Yet if it is not simply discarded, it is because the alternative — a 'conjunctural' view of truth as pragmatist and provisional, a mere cluster of passing interests — is too close to Lovelace for comfort. For there is no doubt that his political violence is intimately linked to his epistemological scepticism and 'deconstructive' style. Linguistic lawlessness is the other face of his sexual libertinism: a writing which brooks no closure is a desire which knows no mercy. His fertile productivity as author, conjuring fiction out of fiction with effortless *brio*, is the barren epistemology of one for whom truth is whatever instruments of oppression he can breezily assemble, whatever profitable mystification he can momentarily improvise. Lovelace can unfix a sign as deftly as he can break a hymen, 'differencing' with all the delight of one to whom any woman's identity is purely indifferent. It falls to the bourgeoisie, then, to stem the profligate force of the aristocratic pen and penis by effecting a moral closure. It must deploy its own countervailing ideologies of truth, representation and the unitary subject against this deathly dissemination. No reading of the novel which ignores this historical necessity in the name of *écriture* can fail to be moralistic. But though Lovelace is not allowed to deconstruct that bourgeois ideology, he does, after all, powerfully challenge it. Two centuries or so before our current altercations over 'transcendental' and 'deconstructed' subjects, stable sign and floating signifier, Richardson had cast a critical eye on both sides of the argument. If he plumped firmly for one, it was not without awareness of what sacrifices of *jouissance* that option entailed, what rich reaches of subversive wit it excluded. There is no way in which the creator of Lovelace could have felt other than deeply ambiguous about the sober Clarissa, lovingly though he endorsed her. It seems unthinkable that Richardson could have fashioned Lovelace without considerable unconscious guilt: the very fact that he could think his thoughts put him beyond the ideological closure that is Clarissa. His affirmation of Clarissa's world may thus be in part expiatory. Of course Lovelace is only a fiction — indeed trebly so, a literary character who sometimes sees himself as such and is a gripping story-teller in his own right. The novel exploits this fictional status, allowing us to enjoy him as a character while rejecting him as a 'real' man. But that Lovelace is fictional is no true expiation of guilt, for fiction is itself a guilty enough affair. Lovelace worries his author not only because he is a dissolute aristocrat but because he is a type of the writer, and the two figures are disturbingly interrelated. Richardson's own plots, after all, have no more substance behind them than Lovelace's fantasies: his narratives are as arbitrarily self-generating as Lovelace's sexual devices. Indeed it is possible to read Lovelace's pathological pursuit of the 'real' of Clarissa as an allegory of the writer's hunt for an essential truth — a truth which fragments with each new paragraph. 'The real is not representable,' writes Roland Barthes, 'and it is because men ceaselessly try to represent it by words that there is a history of literature... literature is categorically realist, in that it never has anything but the real as its object of desire; and I shall say now, without contradicting myself... that literature is quite as stubbornly unrealistic: it considers sane its desire for the impossible.'[89] What Richardson needs, to ground his writing in truth and purpose, is the closure of Clarissa; but at the level of narrative it is just this closure — Clarissa's refusal to be seduced — which keeps Lovelace as a character in business, providing the generative mechanism of the entire text. The novel's 'guilt', then, is that the more it protects its heroine's virtue, the longer it is able to indulge its 'hero'. Lovelace and Clarissa are complicit as units of textual 'grammar', however 'semantically' antithetical they may be.

Lovelace, however, cannot ultimately be indulged: the political price is too high. Richardson does not allow the unconscious to seduce him from the primacy of class struggle. The coherent bourgeois subject must be affirmed, and *jouissance* consciously sacrificed, if ruling-class rapacity is to be defeated. The tragic irony of the text is that it can ensure the victory of Clarissa only by fetishizing her, as

---

89 Lecture in Inauguration of the Chair of Literary Semiology, Collège de France, *Oxford Literary Review*, Autumn 1979, p. 36.

Lovelace does, to the miraculously integral phallus. Only by aggressively repressing the woman can it aggressively cut down the man; woman as madonna is the only response to woman as whore. Anagrammatically, it is possible to produce either 'a whole' or 'a whore' from 'Harlowe', but neither without leaving an excess. If the aristocracy cannot be opposed by a call for sexual emancipation, it is not only because such a call would be anathema to bourgeois puritanism; it is also because the aristocracy has itself parodied and discredited that solution. Its crime is not only that it oppresses women, but that in doing so it practises a debased version of a *jouissance* which some have argued is properly their own. The 'feminine' excess, fluidity and bodiliness of Lovelacian writing forces femininity itself into the protective enclosure of the masculine. It forces it, that is to say, into the equally intolerable clutches of middle-class patriarchy, in a contradiction at once deadlocked and symbolically defeated in the dying body of Clarissa. There can be no intercourse between Clarissa and Lovelace, no relaxing of this historically vital opposition between fetishism and fluidity, the impossibly self-identical and dangerously diffusive self. They exchange only in the very letter of Richardson's text — that seamless fetish of a novel alive with subversive force.

Whatever the ideological option of a Richardson, *Clarissa* still poses an acute problem for us. Not a problem *consciously* posed by the text, but one that it can be persuaded to raise by a certain reading. For we can surely accept neither the 'imaginary' selfhood of a Clarissa nor the oppressive opportunism of a Lovelace. Put another way, we can endorse neither the deconstructive reading of a Warner nor the liberal humanism of a Kinkead-Weekes. For Kinkead-Weekes, whose love for Clarissa seems to fall not far short of Richardson's own, what the novel finally vindicates is the inviolable mystery of the individual. It is not only that this reading is unhistorical, abstracting some changeless pith of selfhood from the variable historical ways in which subjects are constructed; it is also that it fails to note the irony that such spiritual individualism is the acceptable face of the very system which kills Clarissa. In this sense the novel sees further than its critic: it certainly sees that such individualism is no *answer* to social contradictions. For Kinkead-Weekes, writing at a later stage of class society where such spiritual individualism has successfully identified itself with the 'human' as such, social contradictions would seem no more than the setting for some timeless moral drama. In the world of *Clarissa*, the final exercise of 'free' individual choice is in fact a tragic option for self-extinction. Clarissa is a living contemporary for Kinkead-Weekes, but only because he has abolished history altogether. He is as unable to historicize his liberal humanism as Warner is to distance his deconstructionism. Kinkead-Weekes is right to see that the novel affirms the 'inviolability of personality', but uncritically assimilates that concern to the ephemeral pieties of twentieth-century liberalism. (The fact that he would no doubt be concerned to learn that his book was 'ideological', as Warner no doubt would not, simply testifies to the difference between long-established prejudices and brashly emergent ones.) The 'integrity of the human person' is indeed preserved, but, as Raymond Williams adds, 'fanatically' so; the unflawed identity which Kinkead-Weekes applauds is a fetish. Warner certainly sees this, and with a vengeance; but he is blind in his turn to the necessities of eighteenth-century class struggle. What Kinkead-Weekes fails to recognize is that there are more ways than one of imagining the 'inviolable' self. His own image is unreservedly essentialist: the immaculate mystery beneath the skin. But the 'inviolable' is also that which slips through the net of signification: that desire which never achieves final definition, not because it is magically at one with itself but because it is always self-divided. *Clarissa* shows us that there is no way of thinking the unity of the self without reckoning into account the unconscious. This is not to belittle 'humanism': it is merely to recognize that it is a project still to be constructed, not a received set of liberal shibboleths. For those today concerned as Richardson was with social transformation, there can be no cavalier dismissal of the 'human', 'closure' or the 'unified self', to be dispersed at a touch of deconstruction. Such notions remain as politically vital for us as they were for Samuel Richardson. What is *Clarissa* but a warning that the trading of such imperatives for the short change of eroticism and *écriture* delivers you to the political enemy? Yet Clarissa is sacrificed anyway, inviolable or not; and this in turn should expose the political defects of a theory of the subject which rests content with coherence and closure, refusing that satirical question mark that is Lovelace.

Richardson's 'fanaticism', according to Williams, is a matter of abstracting sexuality from the whole social process. This, for so finely Lukácsian a critic, is a curious judgement on *Clarissa*, whatever its relevance to *Pamela*. For *Clarissa* superbly 'totalizes' the sexual and the social, conscious of what we might today call the 'relative autonomy' of sexual oppression while materialist enough to discern its economic basis. Sexuality, far from being some displacement of class conflict, is the very medium in which it is conducted. In one sense, the novel does indeed sharply counterpose social relations and sexuality: Clarissa has the unenviable choice of becoming a pawn in the Harlowes' property game or Lovelace's erotic object. Yet this contradiction between bourgeois property and aristocratic anarchy conceals a deeper complicity. Both display a form of possessive individualism. If Lovelace and the Harlowes are ideological antagonists, they are nevertheless part of the same ruling-class power bloc; the Harlowes object to Lovelace not primarily because he is sexually immoral but because he threatens the marriage deal which might elevate them to the nobility. In material terms, the tragedy of Clarissa is not 'world-historical' but a storm in a teacup; it dramatizes a collision between two wings of the eighteenth-century ruling class whose true destiny lay not in conflict but in alliance. In ideological terms, however, the tragedy is indeed of 'world-historical' proportions, a key phase of English class history. Lovelace is a reactionary throwback, an old-style libertine or Restoration relic who resists a proper 'embourgeoisement'; the future of the English aristocracy lies not with him but with the impeccably middle-class Sir Charles Grandison. The death of Clarissa is the mechanism of his downfall, and in that sense the triumph of bourgeois patriarchy. Yet the death, as we have seen, is a two-edged sword: it cannot cut down Lovelace without mutilating the Harlowes too. No Harlowe-like critique of Lovelace is fully possible, for it was they who forced their daughter into his arms in the first place. It is for this reason, not on account of an undue specializing of class crisis to virginity, that the novel has finally nowhere to turn but to Clarissa herself. Her dying encompasses both aristocracy and bourgeoisie, revealing their true unity of interests. Lovelace, as Jean H. Hagstrum has suggested, represents a cynical Hobbesian deflation of middle-class sentimental hypocrisy; but having used him to discredit that ideology, the novel will then use Clarissa in turn to discredit him.

The death of Clarissa is, of course, a deeply ambiguous affair. On the one hand, as Williams rightly argues, its utter refusal of compromise is 'the reverse of consolidation, of the necessary settlement, the striking of a bargain between advantage and value'.[90] It is thus a death against the grain of history, an inversion of *Pamela*, an implacable negation of property and progress. Indeed, writing *Clarissa*

90 *The Country and the City*, p. 65.

seems to have retrospectively revised Richardson's views of his earlier novel: 'It is apparent by the whole tremor of Mr B.'s behaviour,' he writes in a letter of 1749, 'that nothing but such an implicit obedience, and slavish submission, as Pamela shewed to all his injunctions and dictates, could have made her *tolerably* happy, even with a *reformed* rake.'[91] On the other hand, nothing could be more meekly masochistic than this aggressive onslaught on the whole social system, nothing more pacific than Clarissa's resolute turning of her face to the wall. It is by forgiving the aristocrat that she vanquishes him: her victory takes the form of a spiritual submission of which he himself is incapable. The death is a kind of psychical device whereby the novel throttles back its own social aggression, turns it around and lets it lash itself quiet on the body of Clarissa herself. If the bourgeoisie are to attain spiritual hegemony over the squirearchy, this is an essential inversion: you must not fight the class enemy with his own weapons, and the fact that the bourgeoisie are in practice indistinguishable from their superiors on this score counts heavily against them. Clarissa's forgiveness of Lovelace thus reflects something of the bourgeoisie's impulse to make peace with the traditional ruling class; but it also of course frustrates it, since, given her death, no actual alliance will ensue. There is a similar ambivalence in her relationship to bourgeois patriarchy. On the one hand, her death is the strongest conceivable affirmation of that ideology: it is less Lovelace's rape, than the melancholy into which she is plunged by her father's curse, which causes her to die. Clinically speaking, Clarissa dies of depression: unable to live in the knowledge that her obnoxious family have cast her out, she sinks into profoundly masochistic guilt.[92] But her every refusal to condemn the

91 *Selected Letters*, p. 124.
92 Otto Rank has suggested that if Don Juan's infantile sexual

Harlowes, her saintly internalizing of such aggression, blackens them a little deeper in the reader's eyes. If they execrated a daughter as merciful as this, their chances of heaven must indeed be slim. In this sense, the more Clarissa slips into false consciousness, the more admirable she becomes; Richardson is able to let us see that she is both lovable and mistaken, playing off her lowly self image against her objective significance. The 'objective guilt' of the raped woman merges with the 'objective guilt' of the traditional tragic scapegoat, who though innocent assumes the sins of the community. The more virtue is at odds with truth in humbly maligning itself, the more it shames its oppressors. The two uneasily coexisting aspects of Richardson's own sensibility — his Christian piety and social aggressiveness — are brought into devastating interaction.

Perhaps the critics have disliked Clarissa's 'unconscionable time a-dying' (Johnson) because it is not really very realistic. (One might, incidentally, counter Johnson's jeer by pointing out that Clarissa is most impressive not for her protracted death but for the fact that she survives as long as she does.) Mark Kinkead-Weekes has no particular objection to the death on this score, but the title of his study — *Samuel Richardson, Dramatic Novelist* — is

---

regressiveness is forever frustrated in its search for the mother's body, the more successful form of regression in the legend is death itself, which has a similar goal: 'The devouring animals of the underworld, the grave, and the coffin are clearly unambiguous mother symbols' (*The Don Juan Legend*, p. 96). It would seem, then, that *Clarissa* 'splits' these two forms of regressiveness between its two protagonists. Rank's remarks on the ambivalent attitude of the daughter to the murderer of her father are also perhaps relevant to Clarissa's attitude to Lovelace: the daughter 'partly welcomes the murderer as a liberator and a new beloved, and partly scorns and persecutes him as a weaker substitute for the lost primal object' (p. 101).

nevertheless significant. Post-Leavisite criticism likes its
fictional 'ideas' to come in subtly dramatized, psycho-
logically plausible form; whatever is not instantly soluble
in the textures of 'lived experience' is suspect as dryly
theoretic. From this viewpoint, however, *Clarissa* appears
less and less realist the further one steps back from its
relentless detail, in a reversal of those representational
canvases which dissolve as you approach them into streaks
and blurs. In fact the more scrupulous the realism grows
the less realist it is, since the more ludicrous it becomes
that anybody could have written so many letters and still
found time to eat. (Lovelace has been estimated to have
written 14,000 words in a single day.) 'Did I, my dear, in
what I have repeated, and I think they are the very words,
reflect upon my father?' asks Clarissa anxiously of Anna
Howe.[93] Representational writing must brim itself full
of another's 'very words' if it is to avoid deception, and so
simply veers into an alternative fiction: how could Clarissa
have possibly recalled her father's discourse *verbatim*? The
problem of *Clarissa* in this sense is the problem of how not
to become *Tristram Shandy*. How is it to sustain its dogged
faith in the representational sign through all that welter of
detail, subduing such material to shapely narrative and
causal coherence? It is because the ideology of realism
never falters that the text is as inconveniently long as it is:
the reader must not be shamelessly manipulated *à la*
Sterne, cheated by authorial whim or elision, forced to
complain that this is anything less than the authorized
blow-by-blow account. Yet viewed from a long way off,
the very disproportion of this discourse to what it is
'about' — the rape of Clarissa — has a sort of modernist
smack about it, as language is unleashed in pursuit of a
truth for which it is at once excessive and too meagre. It
is, to adopt Clarissa's own word, a text about 'nothing' —

93   vol. 1, p. 102.

about a female body which, for all one's painstaking rhetoric, can never be represented. Neither the cause nor the object of this discourse can be inscribed within it, for both lead us back to an unconscious on the repression of which the whole top-heavy textual business thrives. Without the repressions of Clarissa and the neuroses of Lovelace there would be no novel at all. *Clarissa* as a text would not need to exist if its author were able to 'know' these submerged realities, rather than be constrained to pursue them in the very act of writing.

The death of Clarissa — that Samson-like act of self-immolation by which she brings her enemies toppling to the ground — is certainly resistant to any purely realist reading. Unswerving in its local verisimilitude, the novel coolly throws to the winds any plausibility of the whole. The apotheosis of Clarissa is a brazenly didactic, allegorical gesture, as unpalatable to narrowly realist taste as *Paradise Lost* or Brecht's *Lehrstücke*. It is a death as scandalous in liteary form as in ideological content. At this historical point, there is no 'realist' way in which the deathly contradictions of patriarchy and class society may be resolved; what we are offered instead is a tragic negation which is, inseparably, utopian transcendence, cutting the knot of all those thwarting realist complexities in a boldly gratuitous gesture which trusts in heaven alone. Raymond Williams sees this as a false displacement, an abstracting of actual history to a 'fallen world' which must be virtuously spurned. Yet if this is doubtless how Richardson and Clarissa view the matter, theirs is not necessarily the last or most authoritative word. What societies cannot yet accomplish historically, they often enough nurture in the realm of myth; and this seems to me the most relevant contemporary reading of Clarissa's religious faith. Williams recognizes that 'there was not, as yet, any available and adequate social response' to this 'basically ruthless social order',[94] but he fails to relate this political insight to Clarissa's supreme trust in God. In the England of 1748, an 'adequate social response' to human exploitation may be as remote as Clarissa's God, but it will also need to be as absolute and all-encompassing. Certainly no mere reformism will suffice to uproot the Harlowes and Lovelaces of history, as the novel plainly enough implies. Clarissa is not, after all, purely narcissistic. As far as she is concerned, she relies not upon her own powers but upon heaven: 'God Almighty would not let me depend for comfort on any but himself.'[95] There is a source of power and solace beyond Clarissa, for which her dying is no merely individualist act but a sign of human solidarity. If for Richardson and his heroine that absent dimension has the name of God, we ourselves, reading the novel after the advent of the women's movement, may perhaps give a more precise name to those sources of power and solace, with the historical emergence of which a modern Clarissa would not need to die.

94 *The Country and the City*, p. 65.
95 vol. 4, p. 339.

Postscript

The 'feminization of discourse' witnessed by the eighteenth century was not a sexual revolution. It was imperative to mollify ruling-class barbarism with the milk of middle-class kindness, but not, naturally, to the point where virility itself came under threat. Male hegemony was to be sweetened but not undermined; women were to be exalted but not emancipated. The recourse to the feminine was always problematical — for how could the public sphere of male discourse model itself upon values drawn from an essentially private realm? How could meekness, chastity, sentiment and benevolence, qualities bound up with the passive, powerless woman, survive transplanting to the political arena?

The answer to this question is Richardson's last novel, *Sir Charles Grandison*. *Grandison* is not just a cashing in on the success of *Clarissa*: it is the logical culmination of Richardson's ideological project, a necessary move in the whole middle-class cultural enterprise. *Pamela* and *Clarissa* have foregrounded the woman, pressing deep into new dimensions of feeling; it is now time for that tide of feminization to be recuperated by patriarchy and centred on a man. If the virtues of a Clarissa cannot be shown to be practicable for a 'man of the world', then they are ideologically barren. If chastity and altruism are no more than a utopian impulse, values proper only to adolescent females, then Richardson has produced fantasy rather than social critique. It is essential at all costs to demonstrate that men, too, can be chaste, pious and pacific without being any the less manly for that. Or, indeed, without being any the less materially successful. What is at stake in *Grandison* is nothing less than the production of a new kind of male subject. If this is a recuperative gesture, raiding the resources of the feminine to 'modernize' male dominance, it is also in its own way an admirable one. For Richardson has grasped the point that the so-called 'woman question' is nothing of the kind — that the root of the sexual problem is men. In the figure of Sir Charles Grandison, then, he will give us a womanly man, for whom power and tenderness are fully compatible.

If this is where the problems are resolved, however, it is also where they begin. For Grandison is not only a womanly man; he is also, in Leslie Stephen's phrase, a prig of the first water. His ludicrously unflawed virtue makes him less an eighteenth-century baronet than a Jesus Christ in knee-breeches, a dreary paragon of goodness delivering moral platitudes which a shorthand writer concealed in a nearby closet transcribes for posterity. (He is, however, considerate enough to consult his watch from time to time during his drawing-room homilies.) The other characters, as Eaves and Kimpel comment, 'fall into raptures at [his] slightest civility',[1] singing his praises in entranced hyperbole. For Stephen, he is 'one of those solemn beings who can't shave themselves without implicitly asserting a great moral principle';[2] for William Hazlitt he was, quite simply, 'the prince of coxcombs'. Walter Scott tells of an old lady who chose to hear *Grandison* read to her in preference to any other work, as she could fall asleep and wake up again

1 *Samuel Richardson*, p. 394.
2 Introduction to *Samuel Richardson: Works* (London, 1883), p. xxxix.

without missing anything of the story.[3] Responding to a defence of the novel's realism, Eaves and Kimpel, not noted for their swingeing iconoclasm, remark that 'One is *there*, certainly; but one would rather be somewhere else.'[4] A weighty objection to Sir Charles is not just his tedious perfection, all the way from his 'fine teeth' to his charitable refusal to dock his horses' tails, but the fact that he ousts the novel's heroine, Harriet Byron. Before Grandison makes his glacially virtuous entry, Harriet is an engagingly shrewd, intelligent and independent woman, brave enough to argue the uses of learning with a supercilious Oxford don, and acidly perceptive of male absurdities ('He again vowed his passion, and such stuff'). For the rest of the novel — a considerable span — she is effectively reduced to Grandison's unrequited lover, defined largely in relation to him.

The unreality of Grandison is clearly more than a technical failing. It indicates a genuine ideological dilemma. For though Grandison solves a problem by blending male power and feminine virtue, it is clear enough to us that he can exercise such virtues precisely *because* he has power — because he is a paternalist patriarch with a steady flow of cash, deserving poor and faulty friends to be regularly overwhelmed by his forgiveness. This, however, makes him something less than the novel's ideological project really demands. For the full inscription of 'feminine' values in the public sphere would logically require a figure more resolutely public than Grandison actually is. He is no battling bourgeois but an aristocrat semi-withdrawn from social life, whose stomping ground is his circle of fawning friends and romantic overseas entanglements rather than court or city. His virtue is a matter of private benevolence rather than political action, and this is one reason why it

3 Quoted in *Samuel Richardson*, p. 389.
4 *Samuel Richardson*, p. 390.

remains so miraculously undented. To consummate his
project, Richardson is constrained to produce a hero who
is in some sense a social throwback, faintly ill at ease in
contemporary society despite his social graces, given to
denouncing the age as 'effeminate'. The implication of
all this — that actual society is an oppressive area where
virtue and success are not so smoothly compatible — then
runs as an interrogative undertone throughout the text.
Grandison 'socializes' the virtues of *Clarissa*, but is ironically a less social novel. Because of its semi-private nature,
Grandison's goodness can be put to no radical test, and
so remains unreal. It is not a question of the supposed
impossibility of portraying virtue convincingly: what else
is Clarissa? It is rather that Clarissa's virtue is dramatized
dialectically, locked in minutely detailed conflict with
ruling-class oppression. If she is a utopian image, it is of
a negative kind: the saintliness of her dying is acceptable
because it is consciously otherworldly, a purity untenable
in public life and so a deliberately 'staged', non-realist
critique of that life. Because she is ideal, Clarissa cannot
survive; Grandison's goodness helps him to flourish in
this world, as much a spur to his success as it was a tragic
obstacle to it for Clarissa. Yet he flourishes only because
the novel protects him from major conflict, and so empties
itself of an aggressiveness crucial to Richardson's art.
Grandison is forced to suppress sexual and class dialectics
in the name of ideological harmony: the abduction of
Harriet Byron by a villainous aristocrat is a kind of crude
cartoon re-run of *Clarissa*, a hollowly melodramatic affair
in which nothing whatsoever is at stake. The self-affirmative
irreverence of a Pamela or Anna Howe is harmlessly
channelled into the rather too free tongue of Grandison's
sister, Charlotte. Grandison is a baronet, the lowest of the
hereditary orders, and this underscores his closeness to the
upper bourgeoisie. If the text aims to synthesize gender
roles, it equally aims to quell the class conflicts of *Pamela*

and *Clarissa* by uniting bourgeoisie and nobility in the person of an impeccably middle-class aristocrat. The *longueurs* of the novel — its notorious inability to whip up any narrative less trivial than love-imbroglios — is the price it pays for this deliberate closure.

The chief reason for the novel's weakness, however, has to do with the nature of patriarchy itself. Where *Grandison* is most progressive is in its massive strike against the 'double standard': having written a novel about a chaste woman, Richardson will now show how such chastity is equally essential for men. But this liberal even-handedness merely obfuscates a deeper sexual inequality. For the blunt truth is that in patriarchal society it does not *matter* whether men are chaste or not. Grandison's virginity has no price, no exchange value: unlike Clarissa, he is not a commodity on the sex and property market. Clarissa will end up by withdrawing herself from such circulation; Grandison, as a man, is never in circulation in the first place. Whether he marries Harriet or Clementina is merely a question of 'romantic' interest: it engages no substantive historical issues, as does Clarissa's marriageability. His virtue is no more than a personal affair, nobody's business but his own. In this sense, the novel is in a precise sense moralistic: by choosing a man as its centre, it is forced to dissociate moral questions from political power structures. *Clarissa*, heavily sententious though it sometimes is, is not at all moralistic in this sense: because its protagonist is a woman, her moral and sexual life is bound to engage some of the most material issues of the epoch. Jane Austen, having written her play on Sir Charles,[5] had then to shift direction to become the major novelist she did: rapidly retreating from this cul-de-sac, she put Harriet Byrons rather than Charles Grandisons at the centre of her works.

5 See *Jane Austen's 'Sir Charles Grandison'*, transcribed and ed. by Brian Southam (Oxford, 1981).

Simone de Beauvoir remarks in *The Second Sex* that in a patriarchal society what matters is what a woman *is* and what a man *does*. *Clarissa's* triumph is to confirm the first part of this judgement; *Grandison's* ironic achievement is unwittingly to demonstrate the truth of the second. The simplest possible contrast between the two novels lies in the fact that Grandison cannot be raped. The novel thus dramatizes a major contradiction: its genuinely progressive drive to generalize the discourse of femininity to men exposes, in the very thinness of the text, an insurmountable sexual difference.

'Men and women are brothers and sisters,' wrote Richardson, 'they are not of different species.'[6] He believed that marriage should mean companionship rather than female slavery, but thought a wife should never be independent of her husband; he held that women should be educated, but thought them good for nothing if they neglected their domestic duties. He was called 'Guardian of the female sex' by a woman friend, and battled against what he saw as a fashion to depreciate women; he also constrained two of his 'sisters' to waste their lives in bearing him twelve children, only four of whom survived infancy. Richardson's importance for contemporary feminism, then, lies not in his cautiously progressive views of gender, but in the way in which one of his novels transformed that ideology well beyond its limits, and the way in which another, however thinly and recuperatively, sought to

6 *Selected Letters*, p. 297. Richardson's liberalism had its limits, however: the cast list of *Grandison* is divided into 'Men, Women, and Italians'.

generalize the discourse of women to the production of a new male subject. The contradiction of *Sir Charles Grandison* is that its blending of genders is inseparable from a synthesis of classes which simply reproduces sexual oppression. Richardson's importance lies also in his bold experiments with form: the shift from 'language' to 'discourse' belongs with the transition from masculine to feminine and aristocracy to bourgeoisie. If much of the ideology embodied in that discourse is not, for us, acceptable, the techniques of literary production in which it is inscribed remain politically resourceful and suggestive.

That Richardson is in these ways a contradictory figure is evident enough in the two antithetical literary currents which flow through him. The consolidated class settlement of *Sir Charles Grandison*, the tale of the soberly embourgeoisified aristocracy, will pass straight into Jane Austen and the novel of social manners, as a literary instrument of English ruling-class hegemony. In this sense, Richardson helped to perfect an ideological form for the very class towards which he felt so ambivalent. But there is also a more radical current flowing through Richardson, which can be traced all the way from eighteenth-century women's writing, resurfaces explosively in the 'female Gothic', finds its major articulation in the Brontës and passes on to the women's writing of our own time. It is perhaps in part because Richardson is an indispensable moment of this emancipatory movement that the rape of Clarissa has been so ritually re-enacted by generations of critics.

Index